IDEAS FOR CHILDREN'S WRITERS

If you want to know how . . .

Writing a Children's Book
'Rarely have I seen such well laid out advice and information –
don't take my word for it, buy a copy and see for yourself . . .
Highly recommended' – *Writers' Bulletin*

Creative Writing
'This is a book which merits a place on every writer's booklist'
– *Writers' Bulletin*

Writers' Guide to Copyright and Law
'Utterly invaluable . . . an absolute must for anyone putting pen to
paper for publication' – A reader, Leicestershire, UK

howtobooks

For full details, please send for a free copy
of the latest catalogue to:
How To Books
3 Newtec Place, Magdalen Road
Oxford OX4 1RE, United Kingdom
email: info@howtobooks.co.uk
www.howtobooks.co.uk

IDEAS FOR CHILDREN'S WRITERS

A comprehensive

resource book of

plots, themes,

genres, lists,

what's hot &

what's not

PAMELA CLEAVER

howtobooks

Published by How To Books Ltd,
3 Newtec Place, Magdalen Road,
Oxford OX4 1RE, United Kingdom.
Tel: (01865) 793806. Fax: (01865) 248780.
Email: info@howtobooks.co.uk
http://www.howtobooks.co.uk

First published 2006

British Library Cataloguing in Publication Data.
A catalogue record for this book is available from
the British Library.

Produced for How To Books by Deer Park Productions, Tavistock
Edited by Sharika Sharma
Cover design by Baseline Arts Ltd, Oxford
Typeset by Kestrel Data, Exeter, Devon
Printed and bound by Cromwell Press Ltd, Trowbridge, Wiltshire

NOTE: The material contained in this book is set out in good
faith for general guidance and no liability can be accepted
for loss or expense incurred as a result of relying on particular
circumstances on statements made in the book. Laws and
regulations are complex and liable to change, and readers should
check the current position with the relevant authorities before
making personal arrangements.

Contents

Acknowledgements

Lots of people helped me with this book, making suggestions, brainstorming ideas, checking certain sections and allowing me to quote them. Any mistakes are, however, my own. So a thousand thanks to:

Paeony Lewis, Darren Andrews, Arabella Lane, Jamie Lane, George Cleaver, Rupert Cleaver, Carla Cleaver, Sean Mardling, Lisa Mayfield, Roxanne Richardson, Leslie Mendoza, Stephen Bowden (who always knows everything: private joke), Dotti Enderlie, Kate Allan, Elizabeth Chadwick, Rosemary Laurey, Eileen Ramsey, Ian Ramsey, Angela Robinson, Sharika Sharma, Terie Garrison, Benita Brown and Margaret Pemberton.

I am deeply indebted to my son Rupert (www. traversgfx.com) who arranged the illustrations for me and was always ready with computer advice.

Special thanks to online groups who gave me support and encouragement: FAW, JCW, UKnovelists, romna and word-pool.

Introduction

According to Nielson BookScan just under 35 million children's books were sold in the UK last year and it is projected there will be even more this year. I am sure you want your book to be one of them, so I have written *Ideas for Children's Writers* to help you. In *Writing a Children's Book* I said that I was happy to answer questions relevant to subjects raised in the book; using some of those questions and going a step or two further than in my previous book I have put together this new one.

I hope it will help you with many aspects of writing your story. There are lists of attributes to help you create interesting, believable characters; lists of plots and themes; genres – what's hot and what's not; locations and how much description to use. There is a list of frequently asked questions about approaching publishers and submitting manuscripts; I tell you what to expect if your book is accepted, and what to do if it is not.

To save you time in researching, there are lists of things you might want to know, ranging from dates of the kings and queens of England, through quarantine and incubation time for childhood illnesses to emoticons and short forms for text messaging – and some fun things.

Please note that throughout the book I use male pronouns for clarity and to avoid clumsiness. If you find these offensive, please feel free to substitute female ones where appropriate.

As before, I am willing to answer questions arising out of the book; write to me at pamelatcuk@yahoo.co.uk. However, I regret I cannot read manuscripts and give opinions on them – I am too busy tutoring and doing my own writing.

Pamela Cleaver,
Norfolk, 2005

Limbering Up

Before you tackle writing a story, here are some exercises and ways of thinking about writing for children that you may find helpful. You are going to need a good sized notebook in which to do the exercises, as well as a pocket notebook that goes everywhere with you in which you jot down impressions, thoughts, book titles, newly discovered words, and story ideas. Somerset Maugham said in *A Writer's Notebook*:

For my part I think to keep copious notes is an excellent practice . . . They cannot fail to be of service if they are used with intelligence and discretion.

YOU ARE YOUR OWN BEST RESOURCE

For a children's writer, his best resource is himself when young. OK, so times and customs have changed, but the essential feelings of children have not. Your best resource for child characters is yourself. Find photos of yourself at 5 (starting school), 11 (moving to senior school) and 13 (becoming a teenager), and ask yourself some questions.

◆ What were you like? Did you change a lot between these three landmark ages?

Me at ages 5, 11 and 13

- What did you want at each of these ages? Did you just want to fit in or did you want to be different from your peers?

- If you are one of several brothers and sisters, think about your relationship with the others. Do you fit into the stereotypical pattern in families: eldest child – a leader, the responsible one; second child – competitive, always trying to catch up to older sibling; middle child – the contrary one, always crying, 'It's not fair!'; the youngest – petted and spoiled, bullied and badgered by turns.

- If you are an only child, did you enjoy being the centre of attention or did you want brothers and sisters, and if so, why?

- What would you have liked to have been like rather than what you were? Would you have liked to have been good at games? Clever? Brave? Popular?

- Would you have liked to have been an orphan (think of Harry Potter, Molly Moon and Tracy Beaker) so you didn't have parents who interfere? It's a vexed question in children's books whether to have parents out of the way, or to have them present. Usually, the younger the character, the more important parents are.

MAKE SOME LISTS

- List important events in your childhood. They might range from your going to hospital to winning a cup, or failing an important exam. How did you feel about it at the time? What were the consequences? Could you, by altering and embroidering any of these events, make a story?

◆ List places that were important to you as a child – where you went on holiday; grandma and grandpa's house; a castle or museum that you visited and which struck you as amazing, wonderful or interesting. Perhaps there was a den you and your chums built that was the focus of your lives. It may surprise you when thinking of these places how many long forgotten details come to mind. Remember and note down those details, details are what make a place come alive for readers.

◆ Think of the house you lived in and describe it as you saw it as a child, not the way you would see it now. Remember, things that seem small and commonplace to an adult may seem huge and perhaps intimidating to a child. Were there places that seemed forbidding as well as places that seemed welcoming and cosy? What was it like for you?

◆ Think of the people who loomed large in your childhood apart from parents and grandparents: certain teachers (the nasty ones as well as the nice ones); people in your class; children you played with; neighbours; imposing friends of your parents. Was there someone you hated? Make character sketches of any of these people if you think you could use them (suitably disguised) in your writing.

◆ What were you scared of as a child? Remembering your fears, both real and irrational, may give you an idea for a children's story. Writing about it will be cathartic and stories about fears overcome are uplifting and helpful to young readers as well as being popular.

◆ What were your favourite toys? A beloved bear, a precious doll or a super racing bike could feature in a story. Encourage your imagination to embroider and embellish.

◆ What did you long for, but never get at the three crucial ages mentioned earlier? You could either make your character get these items, or learn to do without as you did.

◆ What were your favourite foods? Probably different from today's children's favourites, but food is an important ingredient in writing for children. Remember the meal the children had with Mr Tumnus the faun in C.S. Lewis's *The Lion, the Witch and the Wardrobe,* the delicious food in Frances Hodgson Burnett's *A Little Princess* brought to her attic by Ram Dass when Sarah was starving.

◆ Did you have pets? If so, what sort and what was your relationship with them? Books that focus on an animal, telling its life story are hard to sell, but characters who have pets with personality are popular, and the animals can be used to trigger incidents in your plots. Pets can be the focus of humorous incidents that will appeal to children.

◆ What were your favourite books, and why? Could you take the basic idea, or the part that particularly intrigued you, alter the setting, bring it up to date and create a new story? There is a process called *bricolage* which is taking parts of different stories and using them to make a new one, rather like assembling pieces of fabric to make a patchwork quilt. Remember, there is nothing new under the sun, only new ways of looking at things.

There should be enough material in these lists for you to create a dozen or more stories if you let your mind play with the ideas you have dredged up from your past. Be bold: exaggerate, extrapolate and expand to create something fresh.

USE ALL YOUR SENSES

1. Sight

Writers need to be observant. Look out of the nearest window. What do you see? I'm doing that now. It's a dull day but in front of the window is a crab apple tree full of small red fruits. I see it every day and don't pay much attention to it, but if I take the advice Miss Tick gives to Tiffany Aching (a trainee witch) in Terry Pratchett's *A Hat Full of Sky*, 'Open your eyes, then open your eyes,' – what do I see now? I notice the shape of the tree, I see that the little red crab apples look like hanging rubies. A bird alights and begins pecking the apples, shaking the fragile branches. If I were to describe this tree in a story, my second look would give me more material to play with.

Here is a list of some things you might want to describe. Use it to jog your memory, then create your own list.

Sights

Old houses, castles, churches

New buildings, townscapes

Sun shining on a calm sea

Sea whipped up into angry waves

Blue skies with white clouds

Storm clouds

Colourful sunsets

Young animals – lambs, kittens, puppies and foals

Woodland and forests

Corn rippling in a breeze

Trees outlined in white frost

Christmas trees dressed with fairy lights and tinsel

A crowded market place or mall

2. Sound

You need to open your ears wider than usual too. You need to describe many different sounds when you are writing. Listen to a squeaking door, and try to put into words the sound it makes. Onomatopoeia (words that imitate the sound they describe) is useful here. You hear a dog bark. Does it sound angry or lonely? Music is playing in another room. What kind of music is it? Do you like it or does it get on your nerves? Think of startling noises, and then soothing noises, make notes about them – they will add force to your writing.

Sounds

Rain beating on windows

Wind howling round the house

Music to dance to

Haunting music that touches you

Hammer ringing on an anvil

Hooves of a galloping horse

An engine revving

Helicopter overhead

Church bells

A fanfare of trumpets

A siren

Pneumatic drill

A scream

Bells pealing

3. Touch

Try running your hands over different surfaces. There's the soft velvet of a cushion, the rough surface of a doormat, the smooth feeling of a polished table, the feeling of water running over your hands when you wash, the heat near the stove when a meal is cooking, the cold air when you open a refrigerator door or a freezer. Think of holding a rope or a string that is being pulled tight. Describe it cutting into your hands, and the pain you feel. Tactile writing is vivid and makes readers feel they are right there with the characters.

Touch

Brick and concrete

Silk and velvet

Sandpaper and bristles

Slugs, snails and worms

Rain-soaked clothes after drenching

Hot sand and stones on a beach

The softness of animal fur

Different fruit skins – peach, pineapple, kiwi fruit, orange

Basket work and sacking

The chill of ice and snow

4. Scents and smells

Smell is the most evocative of the senses and the hardest to describe. You either have to compare a smell with something else, or mention something everyone knows so your words bring the scent to mind. In *A Hat Full of Sky,* Terry Pratchett says, 'The nose is a very big thinker. It's good at memory – very good. So good that a smell can take you back in memory so hard it hurts.'

Here is Dodie Smith in *I Capture the Castle*; Cassandra is in church:

Then I remembered what the Vicar had said about knowing God with all one's senses, so I gave my ears a rest and tried my nose. There was a smell of old wood, old carpet hassocks, old hymn books – a composite musty, dusty smell.

Diana Norman in *The Vizard Mask* described the smell of a Restoration theatre dressing room, something we do not know but can imagine from the comparisons:

She was enveloped in a smell compounded of orange peel, baize, fish glue, old scent, tobacco and dust.

Don't ignore unpleasant smells. The smell of over-cooked cabbage hanging in the air, the nauseating, sweetish smell of ether in hospitals, the ammonia stink of fish that has gone off, garlic on someone's breath, the smell of sweat-impregnated clothes that need washing – all these can be used to point up atmosphere in a scene.

Smells

Freshly brewed coffee

Soap

Smoke from a bonfire

Fish

Onions frying

Exhaust fumes

Stables and cow sheds

Old, unwashed clothes

Sweaty socks and shoes

Flower scents: rose, lavender, lily of the valley

Disinfectant

Chlorine in swimming pools

Clean babies and warm puppies

Meat roasting

Incense burning

---

5. Taste

There are four tastes: salty, sour, sweet and bitter. Salt is self-explanatory; lemons and vinegar are sour and make you screw your mouth up. Sugar and all things made with it are sweet, and some medicines like quinine, for instance, are bitter, and so is bad coffee. Food is usually described as 'delicious' or 'disgusting' at the top and bottom of the approval rating of the taste spectrum, with 'bland' in the middle. You may need to describe a variety of tastes in your stories.

Don't forget how closely allied taste and smell are. When you have a head cold, you cannot taste your food. Texture of food is important too. Two members of my family cannot abide anything smooth and slippery such as egg white and jelly, which their siblings love.

One of my favourite descriptions of taste is the liquid Alice drank in Lewis Carroll's *Alice in Wonderland*:

'Alice ventured to taste it, and, finding it very nice (it had, in fact, a sort of mixed flavour of cherry tart, custard, pineapple, roast turkey, toffee and hot buttered toast), she soon finished it off.'

Tastes and textures in the mouth
Salted peanuts, sea water – *salty*
Burnt coffee, quinine, aloes, cranberries – *bitter*
Lemon, vinegar, crab apples – *sour*
Chocolate, ice cream, sugar – *sweet*
Toast, crisps, celery – *crunchy*
Egg white, jelly, avocado – *smooth*
Mashed potato, fruit puree – *mushy*
Toffee, tough meat, gum – *chewy*
Chillies, curry, pepper – *hot*

WEATHER

It is important to use all the senses in your writing, it is also essential to let your readers know what time of year it is and what the weather is like. Scents and sounds are affected by the seasons: in spring in the country the smell of fresh grass and spring flowers can be uplifting and the sound of birdsong adds to the atmosphere of well-being. But a miserable wet spell can spoil all this and your character may feel depressed and disgruntled. In summer, suppose your characters have gone to the beach, the salty tang of the sea air, the hot smells brought out by the sun, and the scent of sunscreen everywhere add to the holiday feeling, but if a strong wind blows off the sea and rain pours down and they are cold, they will feel quite differently.

Don't forget the difference between dark and light, night and day. Imagine going into a house during a power cut. Unseen objects, normally friendly, seem determined to bark your shins or bump your elbow. Think about walking through a wood on a sunny day with the light filtering down through the trees making dappled patterns, then contrast it with walking through the same wood at night when shapes look sinister and the sound of rustling among the leaves presages who knows what?

Make notes on seasonal effects so that when you come to write a winter scene in midsummer, you have references you can use. On a hot, dry day it can be hard to think of grass crisped white by frost, or rainbow colours on the surface of an oily puddle or the fresh smell of a garden after rain. And in winter, will you remember the hot smells of exhaust fumes in a city street during a heat wave, or the scent of newly mown hay in the country unless you noted them down at the time?

Jilly Cooper kept a diary of what she saw on the common near her home while walking her dogs. She noted when certain plants flowered, what birds she saw, how the weather affected the ground underfoot and later she drew on these references when writing her novels. She published these impressions in *The Common Years.*

READING

It is vital that writers read lots of books. It is surprising how many authors say, 'I am so busy writing that I don't have time to read.' They ought to make time. Here are some of the reasons why you should read.

1. You need to be constantly aware of what is happening in the market place. You must sample other writers' books to see what is being published in your field.

2. You should check out other authors so that you don't duplicate plots. Look for 'holes' in the market that you could fill. If an historical novelist finds there are dozens of books set in the Tudor period, she may realise it is time to try a different era.

3. Read well-known authors to learn from them. How do they achieve their effects? How often do they spring surprises? What kind of language do they use? Do they

always end their chapters with a cliffhanger? Learn from the greats how to improve your writing.

4. Read to feed your imagination. Read widely outside your field and on subjects you don't know well. An idea may come from this that will spark a new story.

CONCLUSION

If you have done some of these exercises you will have plenty of fresh ideas to bring to your writing. You may not want to bother because you are itching to get on with a book or story, but don't be impatient; there will come a day in your writing when something you noted down is just what you need to help with a description or a character's reaction.

As Ursula K. LeGuin said:

Everything one writes comes from experience. Where else could it come from? But the imagination recombines, remakes . . . makes a new world, makes the world new.

(2)

Plotting

There was a time when I was asked, 'How do you get your ideas? Where do you get your plots?' I used to say jokingly that there was a little known shop called 'Plots R Us'. Of course there is not, but I have discovered a website that can help you. www.ideas4writers.co.uk is full of helpful ideas. Have a look at it and if it appeals to you you can join them for a small subscription.

However, it is not hard to find plots on your own; ideas for stories are all around you. If your mind is receptive, if you are in what some writers call 'gathering mode' anything can spark a plot idea.

WHAT IS A PLOT?

For our purposes, it is what the story you are going to write is about. People often ask, 'Which comes first? Your characters or your plot?' That's a bit like, 'Which came first? The chicken or the egg?' It depends on what kind of story you are going to write, but in the development of your story, plot and character work hand in hand. The traits and motivation of a character affect the action of the plot, and the things you decide will happen in your plot affect the characters' behaviour.

Character driven plots

These begin with a person. Imagine someone and think about them.

◆ What does he want?

◆ Why can't he have it?

◆ Who or what is standing in his way?

◆ What does he do to try to achieve his goal?

◆ Does he win straight away? (This makes for a very short story and it lacks conflict, so it probably won't work.)

◆ Does he fail, then try again and again? Use the rule of three here. Remember in fairy tales how often the hero tries three times, fails the first two and wins on the third try. This gives the story both rhythm and balance; it has a mythic resonance, and victory the third time is satisfying.

◆ How does his story end? Happy ever after with your hero getting what he wants? Or does he learn to live without it, which is sometimes more realistic and can be just as satisfying, or does it end tragically?

Action-driven plots

These start with an idea that you can build on. Think of an exciting or interesting incident. Let's say you decide a young boy uncovers a conspiracy that threatens his world. This is a good starting point, but you need to ask some questions to flesh out your concept.

◆ Who is the boy who discovers it? (Already character is going to affect your plot.)

◆ Why is your hero involved in this? You must give him strong motivation – loyalty, pride, patriotism, family feeling (perhaps his father is with the king, for instance).

◆ Who is going to help him? Often in this type of story, the hero has a sidekick or helper. It could be someone he meets on his journey as he sets out to deal with the situation or it could be a sibling or a trusted friend. If it is a fantasy it could be a talking animal or a magical personage. If it is science fiction it could be an alien, a computer or a robot.

◆ Who is the antagonist (the villain), the person who will place barriers in the hero's way, who will push against him and try to make his mission fail?

◆ What is going to happen next? You need to plan more action to keep your story going and avoid the dreaded sagging middle that often plagues authors.

◆ Where is this going to take place? Choose your setting. It can be your home town, but it doesn't have to be a real place, you can invent another country, another world. (See Chapter 5, Where and When?).

◆ How does your hero discover the conspiracy? This is your inciting incident and may be the way you start your story.

◆ When is this taking place? You can set it in the past. If you are writing historical fiction, it could be a documented attempt on the life of a real king, as in the Gunpowder Plot. You can set it in the future, in another world; or you can set it in a nebulous time in a fantasy world.

WHAT NEXT?

Remember, a story has three parts – a beginning, a middle and an end.

1. Beginning

We will talk more about beginnings later, but it is best to start a story with one of the following:

◆ on a day that is different

◆ with the arrival of someone (often a stranger)

◆ with a quarrel

◆ where the trouble begins.

The point about the beginning is that it is vital to hook your reader and make it unthinkable for him to put the book down, so even at the plotting stage it is a good idea to decide what kicks off your story.

2. Middle

The middle is where you bring in your two greatest allies: *conflict* and *complications*. You need them to keep the story going and to keep the reader interested. Beware of another C that can spoil your story – *coincidence*. Use it sparingly. Editors are wary of coincidences, and if readers find part of the story hard to swallow, a pound to a penny, it will be because of a gratuitous coincidence.

Here are some conflicts and complications you can use. Fill your stories with obstacles for the protagonists to overcome.

Argument

Bad weather

Death

Deflation

Denial

Disapproval

Discovery

Disillusion

Failure

Serious injury

Mechanical device fails

Mistake

Mystery

New character arrives

Opposition

Problem

Quarrel

Resistance

Surprise

3. The End

For your ending, you will want to have a big scene, which is usually a showdown between the hero and the villain. But just before you get to this, you can raise the tension of your story by having a black moment, when all seems lost and the reader thinks the hero is sure to fail. This makes the denouement all the more exciting. The hero can get over the black moment by:

◆ his own ingenuity

- the help of his sidekick

- sacrificing something important to him.

Don't use ploys like:

- with one bound he was free (beloved of old comic book heroes)

- letting someone else (other than his best pal) produce the solution

- deus ex machina (the god in the car, who in ancient plays was let down from above on a rope, and put everything right)

- our old enemy coincidence.

In the same way, in the big climax, do not let anyone else but the hero be responsible for the triumph. There should be:

- no fortuitous death of the villain

- no adult taking over from our child hero

- no waving of magic wands.

SOME PLOTTING TRIGGERS TO START YOU OFF

Conflict of loyalty
Our hero has to choose between ideas put forward by two friends. Whichever choice he makes, one will be disappointed, or even angry and trouble will develop.

Revenge

You need an inciting incident that hurts the hero; he then plots revenge and perhaps begins to carry out his plan. There are two ways you can go here:

1. he can get his revenge (write this carefully so that you don't lose the readers' support for your hero)

2. he can begin to see things differently and find he doesn't want revenge after all, which allows for a happy ending.

Inferior character overcomes a powerful antagonist

Perhaps children foiling developers: a David and Goliath situation. Children foiling crooks is old hat and unless very cleverly handled won't be looked upon with approval by many editors. Of course the battle between good and evil works well; it is as old as storytelling itself.

Your hero has to battle against an inanimate foe

Climate perhaps, or terrain. Some authors and critics say you always need a human antagonist; if you agree, you can get over this by personifying the inanimate – for instance you could have an Old Man of the Mountains who has power over the mountains against which the hero is battling.

Set up a puzzle or a mystery

Your story will be about a hero and/or heroine solving the puzzle. This can be light-hearted or grim and sinister, according to your fancy and the age group at which it is aimed. I don't advise a search for lost family treasure, a plot that has been overdone in children's books.

Put a feud in place, either within a family or between two families

This will give you a situation which leads to plenty of conflict and could be healed by one of the feuders or by an outsider, leading to a happy ending, or it could lead to tragedy as it does in *Romeo and Juliet.*

Someone makes a mistake and has to rectify it

The mistake could be:

◆ missing an appointment

◆ mistaken identity

◆ adding the wrong ingredient to a spell

◆ pressing the wrong button

◆ saying the wrong thing

◆ an inadvertent wish that brings trouble

◆ not listening properly

◆ not thinking before speaking

◆ jumping to the wrong conclusion

◆ forgetting something important

◆ failing to pass on a message.

If you have an absent-minded character, they can make several of these mistakes in one story.

Give your hero/ heroine a secret

Can your hero keep it? Will he tell someone else? Suppose he tells it and the person to whom he tells it reveals it; how will it affect him? And what will be the outcome? Secrets are always intriguing. You can either ensure that the reader knows what the secret is so that the reader goes through agonies on the hero's behalf, or you can keep it mysterious until the denouement and so pull the reader through the story by his anxiety to find out what the secret is.

Suppose something is lost

Your story would be about a quest to find it. It can be something as simple as a favourite toy for younger children, as vital as a piece of information of national importance, or a lost person or object whose presence is essential to the kingdom. Many fairy and folk tales use the quest as a way for a suitor to achieve the hand of a princess, or to save the kingdom. *The Odyssey*, and *Jason and the Argonauts* use this classic device.

In this type of story, it is important that not only does the hero achieve his goal, but that he learns lessons along the way. In all good stories, the hero/heroine should be changed at the end of the story by what he/she has gone through on the journey through the book.

It does not have to be a fairy tale: you can use quests in a modern setting too, and for young children it can be a simple hunt through the house to find the lost object.

How about hidden or mistaken identity?

A person thought to be insignificant turns out to be important, or the other way round. *Daddy-Long-legs* and *The Princess and the Swineherd* are examples of this.

Rags to riches

Consider a story in which an ordinary, humble person, through his own efforts or through good fortune becomes better off and finds happiness. Examples of this are *Cinderella*, *Great Expectations* and *Jane Eyre*. It is a staple of Hollywood films and many romances.

Voyage and return

How about a story in which an unexpected event takes the protagonist out of his usual surroundings into a strange world and brings him safely home again. *Where the Wild Things Are*, *Alice in Wonderland* and *Robinson Crusoe* are examples of this plot.

Comedy

A plot in which unusual happenings have a comic outcome. Often this type of story is character driven, the main character being a joker or laughable in some way. *Captain Underpants, Horrid Henry* and *The BFG* are examples. Magic gone wrong can be used for comedy too and is often used for younger children.

Tragedy

The main character is motivated by a desire for power, or passion and his actions lead him to destruction and death. *Macbeth* and *King Lear* are prime examples. This plot is less suitable for a children's story, as a happy, or at least a hopeful, ending is usually required, but see comments on the

Lemony Snicket stories *A Series of Unfortunate Events* in Chapter 9, Happy Ever After?

Rebirth
Someone falls under a spell or into the clutches of a dark power and is trapped until an act of redemption releases them and restores them to happiness. *Sleeping Beauty* and *A Christmas Carol* are examples of this.

Overcoming a monster
A story in which a hero or heroine confronts a monster and overcomes it, gaining treasure or a loved one's hand. *Jack and the Beanstalk* and *David and Goliath* fit into this category. A variation on this is *Beauty and the Beast* wherein the monster is transformed by love.

The arrival of a stranger
A stranger arrives, gains the trust of the community, settles a problem and moves on, having affected the lives of everyone with whom he has come into contact. This is often used in films, for example *Shane*, and *The Magnificent Seven,* but not so much in children's stories, except, of course, in *Mary Poppins* by P.L. Travers.

The ugly duckling
An overlooked or down-trodden character is transformed into a winner. *Cinderella, The Tortoise and the Hare* and *David and Goliath* fit into this category.

WATCHPOINT

Things to beware of when planning a story.

♦ Don't have a concept that is too small to bear your story. Don't open the hangar doors with a flourish and bring out a mouse instead of a Boeing 747.

♦ Don't have a theme that is so familiar that the reader says after a few pages, 'Oh, I can see where this is going.'

♦ Don't have characters without depth, that are too predictable; in other words, no cardboard characters but fully rounded human beings.

♦ Don't choose a plot that is a mere copy of another book or a film. Bring a twist, something different to the old plot that makes it unique and your own.

OUTLINING THE STORY

There are two schools of thought about this, the Pantsers (those who fly by the seat of their pants) and the Plotters.

Pantsers: some writers like to start with an idea and a few characters and plunge into the story and see where it leads them. E.B. White, author of *Charlotte's Web* said:

When I start a book I never know what my characters are going to do and I accept no responsibility for their eccentric behaviour. Nor do I worry about what children are going to think about the story. I just go ahead and write it the way I see it.

Plotters: they like to make a meticulous outline which can be a list of scenes – so many scenes to a chapter and so many chapters to the book. They have spreadsheets and scene cards.

Pantsers: don't even like to know the end of the book before they get there. They say they would be bored if they knew just what was going to happen, they like to be surprised by what occurs, and that way they keep the story fresh and can surprise the reader. If you put too much effort and energy into the details of plotting, they say, you become stale like an overtrained athlete.

Plotters: cannot work without knowing the final scene. They say if you know the end, every scene you write works towards it. Some even go as far as writing the last chapter first as Margaret Mitchell did for *Gone with the Wind.*

Neither way is right nor wrong. If one way works for you, that is your path. Experiment with both and you will soon find out which kind of writer you are.

DON'T FORGET YOUR NOTEBOOK

I have a separate notebook for every book I write. There is a page for each character and every time I give him a feature or a trait, I note it down. This means that if Aunt Agatha appears in Chapter 3 but doesn't show up again until Chapter 9 and I've forgotten what colour her eyes are, I can check easily. I note down any scraps of dialogue that I may think of when I am not at my desk. That notebook goes everywhere with me. If I have a good idea about something that may happen later, I make a note of it. Each chapter has its own page and after it is written, I jot down a brief summary – this is helpful at the end when I am writing a synopsis.

WRITE A BLURB FOR YOUR STORY

This, which is either the short description of the book on the inside flap of a dust cover, or the summary on the back of a paperback, can be useful in clarifying your thoughts and your purpose. Try to encapsulate the story you are going to write like this:

> WHEN *something happens* (your inciting incident)/ *protagonist* (name)/PURSUES *a goal* (what the protagonist wants). BUT WILL HE SUCCEED WHEN *name of antagonist*/puts obstacles in the way (list some exciting incidents)?

To take the idea suggested under 'action-driven plots' earlier in this chapter, the blurb might say:

> When Jeremy Bisson overhears Lord Lionel Vallsey plotting against the king, he sets out to warn his father, the king's general. But will Jeremy succeed when Lionel steals his horse, lets him find a false map to the king's camp, and finally imprisons him?

As you see, in a blurb you don't give away the end, but clarifying the story in this way will probably suggest the end to you if you don't know it already.

You can use this blurb as your route map or to pitch the book to anyone who asks, 'What is your book about?' and you can use it as part of your covering letter when submitting your manuscript. Some children's editors say they prefer this to a full synopsis.

SUGGESTIONS FOR FURTHER READING

The Seven Basic Plots: *Why We Tell Stories,* by Christopher Booker (New York: Continuum, 2005) lists the plots which since literature began have formed the basis of most stories.

Twenty Master Plots and How to Build Them by Ronald B. Tobias, (London: Piatkus, 1995).

3

Story People – The characters in your book

I don't know a single writer who doesn't believe that the most important ingredient in a story is interesting characters. Jack Heffron in *The Writer's Ideas Book* says:

> There's an old rule about writing that says readers won't care what happens in a story if they don't care WHO it happens to.

So, once you have the glimmering of an idea about the story you intend to write, you need to decide on your cast of characters. Plot and character should go hand in hand, as was explained in the last chapter.

CHOOSING YOUR CHARACTERS

As you are a children's writer, you will almost certainly have several children in your cast. Have you noticed that children are always in a hurry to grow up? This may be why they like to read about children a little older than themselves. For your main character, choose someone at the top of your target age range, so if you are aiming your story at 7–11 year olds, an 11- or 12-year-old is an ideal hero, perhaps with a sibling of 7 or 8 to keep the lower end of the range interested.

A mix of boys and girls should be used in stories, and if it is a contemporary story a multi-cultural group of characters to reflect the reality of today's world.

You will probably also need some adults. Will your main character be living at home with his family? If so you need to think about his parents and other relatives who play a part in his life. You need to decide on their background. Are they well-off? Poor? What does the father do for a living? Does the mother work? How does your character get on with his parents? Do they live in a town or in the country? If you are writing a fairy tale, are your characters princes and princesses or are they humble folk? If you are writing a fantasy decide whether your character can do magic or not. If it is science fiction, you will have to create an environment for them (see Chapter 5, Where and When?) All these factors shape your main character's background.

You need an antagonist, someone who can frustrate the hero's aim, who can stand in his way and who will push against him, giving the story conflict and tension. It can be another child or it can be an adult. It need not be an out and out villain – but it can be; the choice is yours. If you are writing a fantasy you have plenty of opponents to choose from – witches, wizards, dragons and any of the fairy folk such as elves, goblins, trolls, or fairies. A good use of your antagonist is to let him discover the hero's weak point and use it against him in any way he can, as often as he can.

YOUR CAST OF CHARACTERS

◆ Don't have more characters than you need. Especially in children's books, too many named characters can lead to confusion. In a class of children all the same age and from similar backgrounds, it can be hard to differentiate Polly from Myrtle unless they are strongly characterised, and you don't want secondary characters to overshadow the protagonist.

◆ Choose your characters for contrast. Build in friction points so that you can have plenty of conflict. Give them a variety of interests.

◆ Don't be too kind to your hero and heroine. You have to give them plenty of trouble to keep your book exciting and to engage the reader's sympathy. For instance:
  ◆ if the hero is relying on his sidekick, make this ally unavailable for that particular incident.
  ◆ if his greatest asset is his ability to run fast, let him sprain his ankle and struggle to overcome it.
  ◆ if he must complete his mission within a certain time, make something happen that shortens the time frame.
  ◆ ask yourself, how could things get worse? Then make the worst thing happen.

NAMING YOUR CHARACTERS

Alfred Bester, the science fiction writer said:

When I start a story, I'm very fussy about names. I read maps and telephone directories. I'm compelled to find or invent names with varying syllables – one, two, three and four. I'm extremely sensitive about tempo, word, colour and context.

What you call your characters is very important. The first contact your reader has with the characters is their name, and the right names give out signals to the reader about the personality of your characters. Keep the names of the main characters simple, save more unusual names for secondary characters. For instance Harry Potter is an 'everyman' name, whereas Draco Malfoy suggests he is an evil character. Try to make the name suit the kind of person you visualise.

◆ Names like Mike, Spike, Dave, Bill and Tom suggest rugged, reliable people; Elaine, Fleur and Colette sound feminine and I wouldn't use any of them for a tomboy – I would choose Jill, Jane or Bess.

◆ Use long names for grand people – three syllable names are impressive: Bernadette, Beverley, Daniella and Griselda for example.

◆ For eccentric characters you can use your imagination and call them something unusual like Farnsworth, Tremayne or Tarkington.

Would you have been so riveted by *Gone with the Wind* if Margaret Mitchell had stuck to her original idea and called her heroine Pansy? I think not: Scarlett O'Hara is the perfect name for her.

An excellent resource for finding names is *The Guinness Book of Names* by Leslie Dunkling, published by Guinness. This not only gives you first names and tells you when they were popular (useful for books set in the past), but also gives you surnames, names for pets, houses, pubs, streets and many other things.

There are several good sites you can consult on the internet.

◆ www.babynames.com is an American site.

◆ www.20000-names.com has a huge selection of names from all around the world grouped under relevant countries, very useful for foreign characters.

◆ www.lowchenaustralia.com/Names.htm specialises in names for pets.

◆ www.notwithoutmyhandbag.com/babynames/index.html is a wacky site that discusses really strange names chosen by parents for their children. Many of these unusual names would be good for fantasy and fairy tale characters.

USING NAMES IN YOUR STORY

◆ Don't have two characters in your story with names beginning with the same letter: this can lead to confusion, even if you vary the number of syllables. If you have Rosy and Ruby in the same scene, you can easily muddle the reader.

◆ If you have a foreign character, don't use the first name that comes to mind. Instead of calling a French boy Jean

Pierre, call him Antoine or Charlot, genuine French names, but less obvious and therefore more striking.

◆ Avoid using names that are the same or similar for boys and girls such as Hilary, Evelyn or Francis/Frances. Nicknames can be confusing too – calling Samantha 'Sam' or Frederica 'Freddie'. Of course, you might do it on purpose to hide the gender of a character, but it is dangerous in stories for younger readers for whom such a ploy may be too subtle.

◆ Vary the number of syllables in your cast of characters. Don't give them all monosyllabic names such as Fred, Alf and Joe. Instead go for Fred, Adrian and Jonathan.

SURNAMES

These need careful choosing too. They can indicate ethnic origin and status.

◆ Short, single syllable names like Smith, Brown and Jones are so universal that you can use them for anybody, but if you were to add a three syllable name and a hyphen, and make Mr Smith Mr Ashington-Smith, it becomes a much grander name. (Do you remember Fotherington-Thomas in the Molesworth books? Not only was it an up-market name, but Fotherington gives a hint of dithering which fitted with his character.)

◆ Names that used to denote trades like Webster, Baker, Potter, Gardener no longer have that connotation and can safely be used for any class of person.

◆ If you are looking for a name for a villain, think of words that start with a harsh combination of consonants – such as Snagge, Scrivens or Skelton, or sound nasty like Goyle, one of Draco Malfoy's henchmen. Skelton might make people think of skeleton which is another good reason for using it. Terry Pratchett is a master of name choosing. Grievous Bodily Harmsworth in *Going Postal* is a perfect name for a thug.

◆ If you are stuck for surnames, use the names of places such as Worthing, Hastings or Guildford. Some village names that consist of two words make splendid double barrelled names – there are several near where I live such as Orton Goldhay, Stow Bedon and Barton Mills. I used Newton Flotman, another nearby village, for a grandee's name and called him Sir Newton Flotman.

CHOOSING NAMES FOR FANTASY CHARACTERS

◆ Don't make them hard to pronounce, this is a stumbling block for a young reader.

◆ Don't make them laughable unless it is a comedy or a story for very young children.

◆ Take an ordinary name and change a letter or a syllable to make it different. Basil can become Baskil, Eric can become Erk, Maureen can become Meenaur and so on.

◆ Don't give a character from the future a name like Xjkrit which no one can pronounce or is likely to remember.

◆ Fairy tale characters can have names as fanciful as you please. I have always liked the name Rosalba in

Thackeray's *The Rose and the Ring*, (which I am sure he made up) although I thought his Prince Giglio in the same story was less effective as it made one think of giggling. Rapunzel and Rumpelstiltskin are wonderful, memorable names.

WHAT DOES YOUR CHARACTER LOOK LIKE?

One way of choosing your characters' appearance is to collect pictures from catalogues and magazines. Boden's children's clothing catalogues use a wide variety of children of various ages that you might find useful as a basis for visualising young characters. Another way to picture characters is to pretend you are casting your story for TV or film, and choose actors who could play the parts.

Be careful about taking characters direct from life, this can get you into trouble if people recognise themselves. But you can use the features of A, the hair of B, the quirks of C, and the height of D. Or you can simply see your character in your mind's eye.

Here are some lists from which you can choose physical features such as hair and eye colour, general looks, inner feelings, where they live and their background. I have included clothes because what people choose to wear says a lot about them. There is a list of hobbies; use this too because having an interest gives a character depth. There is also a list of faults and bad habits, as nobody is perfect, and a flaw makes a character more believable and interesting.

HAIR COLOURS

Blonde
Ash blonde

Golden

Flaxen

Honey coloured

Platinum blonde

Wheaten gold

Brown
Mahogany

Mousy

Nut brown

Black
Blue-black

Colour of a raven's wing

Colour of night

Auburn
Carroty

Conker coloured

Copper

Ginger

Red gold

Titian

Old people's hair
Balding

Grey

Salt and pepper

Silvery

Sparse

White

HAIR STYLES

Afro

Bob

Braided

Buzz cut

Close cropped

Corn rows

Curly

Dreadlocks

Fringe

Flat-top

Long

Pageboy

Plaits

Ponytail

Ringlets

Short back and sides

Skinhead

Straight

Topknot

Wavy

PERSONALITY

Alert

Aloof

Ambitious

Arrogant

Athletic

Brash

Busybody

Careless

Charming

Cheerful

Creative

Curious

Demonstrative

Dreamy

Gentle

Gossipy

Greedy

Gullible

Humourless

Humorous

Imaginative

Impractical

Intelligent

Jealous

Lazy

Loyal

Noisy

Polite

Proud

Quick-tempered

Show-off

Shy

Smug

Sneaky

Sensitive

Stubborn

Suspicious

Whiny

EMOTIONS

Anger

Anxiety

Apathy

Boredom

Confusion

Curiosity

Despair

Excitement

Fear

Fondness

Forgiveness

Friendship

Frustration

Gratitude

Grief

Guilt

Happiness

Hate

Hope

Hostility

Irritation

Jealousy

Loneliness

Longing

Love

Resignation

Restlessness

Sadness

Shame

Surprise

Suspicion

Sympathy

HOME –WHERE CHARACTERS LIVE

Apartment

Bungalow

Cabin

Caravan

Castle

Cave

Chalet

Cottage

Flat

Hotel

House

Houseboat

Hut

Palace

Semi-detached house

Town house

Tree house

PARENTS' PROFESSION

Accountant

Actor

Airman

Architect

Artist

Banker

Baron/Baroness

Cab driver

Chef

Clergyman

Dancer

Dressmaker

Duke/Duchess

Earl/Countess

Enchanter

Engineer

Estate Agent

Gardener

Grand Vizier

Hairdresser

Historian

Horseman/woman

Interior Decorator

Journalist

Judge

King/Queen

Prince/Princess

Lawyer

Model

Musician

Nurse

Policeman/woman

Postman/woman

Sailor

Salesman

Secretary

Shopkeeper

Social worker

Soldier

Sportsman/woman

Spy

Stockbroker

Teacher

Waiter/Waitress

Writer

Undertaker

HOBBIES

Acting

Aeroplane watching

Archery

Ballet

Birdwatching

Boating/sailing

Camping

Card collecting

Computer games

Embroidery

Fencing

Fishing

Gameboy

Jacks

Jigsaw puzzles

Martial arts

Music

Painting

Radio ham

Reading

Record collecting

Scuba-diving

Sports

Stamp collecting

Trainspotting

TV/DVD watching

CHARACTER FAULTS AND BAD HABITS

Arguing

Bad table manners

Casual clumsiness

Cheating

Impatience

Interrupting

Lying

Nail-biting

Noisiness

Nosiness

Quarrelling

Quitting too soon

Rudeness

Selfishness

Showing off

Unpunctuality

Untidiness

Vulgarity

HOW DO THEY TRAVEL?

Aeroplane

Bicycle

Bus

Car

Coach and horses

Four-wheel drive car

Helicopter

Horseback

Lorry

Magic carpet

Motorbike

Ocean liner

Sailing boat

Scooter

Sports car

Train

Van

EDUCATION

Apprenticeship

Boarding school

Comprehensive

Governess/Tutor

Grammar school

Home schooling

Kindergarten

Primary school

Sixth form college

University

CLOTHES

Bikinis

Blouses

Boots

Caps

Dresses

Dressing gowns

Earmuffs

Fleeces

Gloves

Gym shoes

Jackets

Jeans

Jumpers

Mittens

Overcoats

Pyjamas/Nightdresses

Raincoats

Sandals

Scarves

Shirts

Shorts

Swim suits

T-shirts

Ties

Trainers

Vests and pants

Waistcoats

Wellingtons

Woolly hats

GETTING TO KNOW THE CHARACTER BETTER

Now you have decided what your character looks like and what sort of a person he is, you need to get to know him better.

◆ A good way to do this is to write a short statement in the first person as if he were introducing himself to you. 'Hi, my name is William Davies. I am eleven years old and am the oldest in my family . . .' – that sort of thing.

◆ Another way is to write the character's diary for a week: 'Today was awful. Billy Jones, the great bully, caught me outside the gym and grabbed my PE kit and hid it. Of course, Sir didn't believe me when I said someone took it so he gave me detention. He sneered and insisted I'd left it at home. "Lying about it is feeble, Watson," he said.'

♦ Think about your character's most important childhood memory. Most people have something that happened in their past that shapes their present attitude – whether good or bad. Bring it in to show the character's motivation. Perhaps there is something in one of the lists you made, as suggested in Chapter 1, Limbering Up.

♦ Most people, and especially children, have a box or bag in which they keep their treasures. An odd-shaped stone found on the beach; a broken toy that because of its associations is too precious to throw away; a medal that belonged to Grandpa – things like that. What does your character keep and treasure? It can be very indicative.

PUTTING THE CHARACTER ON THE PAGE

Now you know a lot more about your character. How are you going to show this?

1. Description

Don't *tell* the reader everything about him all in one go. Let the details of his appearance and behaviour come out slowly in conjunction with action. Remember the maxim – *show, don't tell*: actions speak louder than words. Don't say, 'Robin's worst fault was being rude to adults.' Have a little scene or incident in which he is asked a perfectly ordinary question to which he gives a disrespectful answer. A little later on when he is shopping for his mother have him treat a shop assistant discourteously. Your reader will know without your telling him that Robin is a rude boy.

2. Dialogue

Everyone has their own way of speaking, they have favourite words, use long or short sentences. Some people are always trying to get a laugh, some show off. Some are hesitant and shy, some overbearing. All these things can be shown in dialogue. As soon as a character starts to talk, you really begin to know him. See the section on dialogue in Chapter 7, Telling the Tale.

3. Action

We have already seen that you can use action to show character traits. The kind of action the hero and/or heroine initiates will be quite different from that initiated by the villain.

4. Reaction

How your character behaves in the face of difficulty, danger, boredom or worry will show the reader what kind of person he is.

5. What other people say about him

This is another way of showing whether your character is good or bad, wise or stupid, brave or cowardly. It is good to have people talking about him.

6. Interior monologue

This is what the character is thinking. Thoughts are very revealing. Someone may be putting on a brave face in a situation while feeling afraid. You can show this by telling the reader what the character is thinking. This is useful too, when people say things, perhaps for politeness' sake, perhaps to be devious, while thinking something else. For example:

> Pat said, 'Thank you. I'd love to come to tea.' *Yuck! You won't catch me going into her house.*

Thoughts can be put in italics as above, or you can write:

> 'Thank you, I'd love to come to tea,' Pat said, but she decided that come what may she would never go into Elfrida's house.

SHOWING CHARACTERS' EMOTIONS

◆ Don't rely on adverbs to convey emotion. Suppose your character is worried. To write, 'Elsa waited anxiously,' is telling. It would be better to show it as in, 'As she waited, pacing up and down the platform, Elsa constantly looked at her watch, frowning as if she couldn't believe time was going so slowly. Would the train ever come? Suppose there had been an accident . . .'.

◆ Don't use clichés to convey emotion. Suppose your character is jealous. The obvious (and wrong) way to express this is, 'When Amanda took the prize, Bella was green with envy.' You would be better off showing Bella's thoughts:

> It wasn't fair, Bella thought. Her picture was just as good as Amanda's. She longed to snatch the prize

from her rival's hands and tell everyone it had been a mistake, that she, Bella, not Amanda, had actually won it.

◆ Make sure you are conveying the exact emotion your character feels. Two characters shouting at each other could convey irritation, anger or hatred. If you wish to convey hatred, be specific:

> Lucy came home from the hairdressers seething. She hoped something horrible would happen to Mr James who had cut her hair so much shorter than she wanted it. Just because she was a child, he should not have disregarded what she'd said. As soon as she got into the house she grabbed her drawing pad and drew a picture of his face showing every loathsome detail – the wart on his upper lip, his mismatched eyes. Her hands shook, so strong was her dislike of him. She took a pair of scissors and cut his face into tiny segments. 'There!' she cried as she threw the pieces on the floor and stamped on them, 'that's the end of you!

SUGGESTIONS FOR FURTHER READING

Character and Viewpoint: Elements of Fiction Writing, Orson Scott Card (Writer's Digest Books, 1988).
Creating Character Emotions, Ann Hood (Story Press, 1988).
www.writers-and-publishers.com/ lists characters' looks and traits.

4

Genres

WHAT'S HOT AND WHAT'S NOT

There is a constant change in the popularity of certain types of books – it is as changeable as the latest fashions in the clothes world. What happens is that a particular book or series becomes a best-seller, and aspiring writers jump on that bandwagon. A few years ago, publishers were clamouring for reality – what they called 'slice of life' books. Then, because the Harry Potter books and Philip Pulman's *His Dark Materials* series were so successful, everyone decided fantasy was the new big thing.

At a recent conference for children's writers the editor of a large publishing house told the delegates that editors are currently buried under mountains of fantasy manuscripts. 'If you have a good story with a good message that ends up fantasy, that's great,' she said, 'but don't set out to write fantasy – it's an editorial turn-off at the moment.' As Carole Blake says in her excellent book *From Pitch to Publication,* 'Too many books on the same subject saturate the market.'

Attitudes and fashions change constantly. When I wrote the first edition of *Writing a Children's Book* in 2000, I said

'Historical novels are currently not popular with readers or publishers.' Five years later the attitude is very different.

WRITE THE BOOK THAT CALLS TO YOU

I am not saying you should ignore the market entirely, that would be foolish, but the books that become classics are books that were written because the author loved the story, and because of that love, produced an excellent book. So suppose there is too much fantasy swilling about in publishers' offices but you passionately want to write fantasy. Go ahead and write it and if the market doesn't want it at the moment, put it to one side and wait for the fashion to change as it assuredly will.

A well-known and much respected author who has been writing children's books for forty years said to me recently that she was putting a good many stories away in a drawer because they were too gentle for today's much edgier market, however she had to write them because she loved the ideas. 'Their time may come,' she said. 'We'll see.'

PICTURE BOOKS

As everyone knows, these are short, highly illustrated books for younger children from 500 to 2,000 words, with a few words on each page. (More on the writing of picture books in Chapter 8, Writing for the Younger Set.)

Market place

Picture books are hard to place unless they are very striking and can be published in other languages besides English. At the moment, publishers are not taking on many new picture book writers, although an exceptional script will always find a home.

FAIRY TALES

These can be divided into two kinds. First are the retellings of traditional stories. Second are new stories in which the background of the fairy tale world remains the same, but what happens there is more in keeping with modern times.

You might, for instance, turn the traditional tale on its head. Instead of a prince or a knight rescuing a damsel in distress, you might have a self-confident maiden rescuing a young man who is in trouble. Or you can pick a story up where the original tale ends and extrapolate from there as Diana Hendry does in *Swan Boy*. This tells the tale of the last of the brothers turned into swans who were saved by their sister making them shirts. If you remember, the last brother's shirt was missing a sleeve so he was left with one arm and one swan's wing.

For examples of modern fairy tales look at Diana Kimpton's Pony-Mad Princess series for which the blurb says:

Princess Ellie is pony-mad! And she's fed up with being a princess! She hates soppy pink dresses and boring waving lessons. She'd much rather be riding one of her four gorgeous ponies, or even mucking out the royal stables.

Market place

Publishers tend to commission well-known authors to retell the traditional tales and are unlikely to take this type of story from a newcomer, but there is a market for well thought out new fairy tales that capture the interest of today's children.

FANTASY WORLDS

This can be a story set in the familiar fairy tale world, this time for the 7–11 age group; a longer book than those designed for younger children as above.

The story can be set in a strange, different world invented by the author as the backdrop for his creation. For instance, the world of Lyra in *Northern Lights* is not our world but the invention of Philip Pullman. In a note on *The Subtle Knife* he says:

> This volume moves between three universes: the universe of *Northern Lights*, which is like ours but different in many ways; the universe we know; and a third universe, which differs from ours in other ways again.

In another kind of fantasy, characters move from our world to another place. Narnia, a magical land entered through a wardrobe, was invented by C. S. Lewis as a setting for his stories.

A close cousin to this is the time-slip; it is our world, but the story starts in the present and goes into the past. For this one, it is important to choose a convincing method of transferring your character from now to then – a thin place in time, a building with a long history, or perhaps the saying of a spell. You can use this type of story to show that the past is not quite as we have imagined it, and having a modern character to comment on it can point up the differences.

Finally, there is our world but with an added ingredient such as magic being the norm and people without magical ability being the outsiders. This is the milieu Diana Wynne Jones uses in several books, and it is used by J.K. Rowling in her books where there are witches, wizards and muggles.

Market place

You will have read in the introduction to this chapter that at the moment editors feel there is too much fantasy struggling for a place in the market, so if you do write fantasy make sure it is different and has something fresh and unusual to offer.

SCIENCE FICTION

Stories set in the future with interesting technology and adventures in space are popular – particularly with boys. Stories with humans trapped inside computer games who have to find a way out or achieve a certain level are another possibility. Younger children like stories with robots and space monsters in them.

Science fiction stories can be used by the author to show what may be the result if certain things happening now in our world (for example, overuse of fossil fuels, cutting down the rainforests and global warming) are not curbed.

Market place

Most children's publishers have sci-fi series and one-offs. Check their catalogues and websites, and consult the current *Children's Writers' and Artists' Yearbook*.

HISTORICAL NOVELS

A few years ago, historical novels were almost impossible to sell, but now well-written, accurately researched historical novels are sought after by publishers, especially if they fit in with the eras and subjects being studied in the various Key Stages of the National Curriculum. Critic Nicholas Tucker suggests that 'the vogue for fantasy has made it respectable to write about things that aren't the present' and children are more interested in history generally now, largely thanks to Terry Deary's *Horrible Histories*. Several publishers have series that purport to be the diary or the adventures of a child who lived through an important historical event such as the Great Fire of London, the London Blitz, the journey of the Mayflower and so on. A thorough knowledge of your period and good research is essential to make these successful.

Market place

If your story fits into the requirements of the curriculum or feeds into a current interest, it will be easier to sell.

ALTERNATIVE HISTORY

These are pseudo-historical novels which take some important turning point in history and postulate what would have happened had the result of a battle or revolution been different. Joan Aiken, for instance, wrote about a world where the Stuarts were on the throne and the Hanoverians were the pretenders.

Market place

There haven't been many of these around lately, but the Aiken books are still popular. Perhaps it is time for a renewal of this type of story.

ANIMAL STORIES

For younger children stories in which animals are the characters and behave like humans are always popular. Family units of Mother Bear, Father Bear and Baby Bear, or stories with animal heroes like Mog the cat, Paddington the bear, and Harry the Dirty Dog work well.

Adventures with animal heroes such as *Time Stops for No Mouse* by Michael Hoyeye, and *The Final Reckoning* by Robin Jarvis in which mice defeat an evil cat, are examples of animal stories for the 7–11 age group. Terry Pratchett won the Carnegie Medal for *The Amazing Maurice and his Educated Rodents*, a story about rats set in his Discworld.

Don't forget dinosaurs. The younger set seem perennially interested in these extinct creatures, and stories about them, both serious and funny, do well.

Dragons are almost as popular as dinosaurs – good dragons and bad dragons seem to be favoured equally.

Market place

All the above types of story will be considered, but what publishers do not seem to want at the moment are biographies of real animals, pets or wild ones. If this is what you want to write, it will have to be exceptional to catch their attention.

REAL-LIFE STORIES

These are the slice of life stories I mentioned in the introduction to this chapter. Jacqueline Wilson is the queen of this type of book which tends to focus on a dysfunctional family, or a child with a problem within the family. Stories about happy families without problems are hard to make interesting.

School stories set in the state school system come under this heading too, and often nowadays seem to focus on bullying. But bullying stories are another area where publishers are becoming swamped with manuscripts using this theme.

Boarding school stories seem to be a thing of the past, although I understand R.L. Stine, popular author of the Goosebumps series, is currently embarking on a new boarding school series.

Sports stories, especially football stories, are popular with boys.

Market place
There is a good market for these stories, especially if you can make them fresh and original.

ADVENTURE STORIES

Ripping yarns, and 'what we got up to on our holidays' were originally the basis of these stories. But as nowadays children are restricted in where they can go without adults, and what they can do (because of parental fears about their safety), imaginary adventures set in an idealised past are a better bet. Pirates are currently very popular.

Market place
Look at publishers' catalogues and websites to see which are taking this type of book. Get onto pirates before that market is saturated.

HORROR AND GHOST STORIES

Both these subjects are winners. I find that horror is sometimes a bit too strong for my stomach, but children like the
right kind of horror. Darren Shan, a prolific horror author,
says:

> A kid reading a scary book is looking to be scared . . .
> This is fun terror. It is not like terror in real life that
> frightens the bejesus out of you.

Thrillers for children are a fairly new on the scene. Anthony
Horowitz writes James Bond type stories with Alex Rider, a
young super spy as hero, which are lapped up by boys. I
picked one up at the library recently and a small boy (about
eight) said, 'My big brother's read that.' 'Did he like it?' I
asked. 'Yeah, but you won't,' he told me, 'It'll be too tough
for you.'

Charlie Higson has started a series of books about the young
James Bond, *SilverFin* is the first and I am hearing praise for
Jimmy Coates: Killer by Joseph Craig. Spy books for boys
may well be the next big thing.

Young children enjoy gentle ghost stories with happy, com-
forting endings, but gore and too much scariness are not for
them.

Market place

Plenty of openings here. Scholastic (a children's book
publisher), for instance, does several creepy series.

YOUNG ADULT AND CROSSOVER BOOKS

This is a huge market and in recent years has become very important. Many adults are reading these books since the success of *His Dark Materials* with grown-ups as well as teenagers. Every publisher wants to have a successful crossover book and is actively looking for them. A recent advertisement encapsulated the ambience when it said: 'For teenagers or adults? It stops mattering on page 1.'

Plots are more complex, themes are stronger and many of the books are darker than we have come to expect from children's books. The sky seems to be the limit as far as subject matter goes. The main constant is a young protagonist. There doesn't even have to be a happy ending, although some kind of resolution is needed.

Hephzibah Anderson in reviewing teenage fiction for the *Observer* said recently:

> Young adult fiction is read only by precocious nine-year-olds and nostalgic young professionals, reaching back to a time when their lives weren't spent toiling in the twilight glow of laptops. Or so my 16-year-old cousin assures me, and there may well be some truth in this. Certainly, the so-called crossover market continues to blossom, with authors commanding healthy, high-profile advances in an otherwise sluggish fiction market.

Market place
Nearly all children's publishers have a range of books aimed at 11- or 12-year-olds and upwards.

CONCLUSION

Choose your genre carefully. Read current books in your chosen category to see what publishers are taking. Be imaginative. Don't write your first idea as soon as you think of it: dig deeper and think harder. Create dynamic characters and vivid settings. Why not try mixing two genres?

SUGGESTIONS FOR FURTHER READING

These books will help you scope out the markets:

Children's Writers' and Artists' Yearbook (London: A & C Black).

The Writer's Handbook Barry Turner (ed.) (London: Pan Macmillan).

Always use the current edition of these books.

www.storypilot.com for sci-fi and fantasy markets.

5

Where and When?

CREATING A WORLD

Sally Beauman wrote:

> In children's fiction there are many worlds that, once encountered, are never forgotten – Alice's underworld, Pook's Hill, Pooh Corner, Toad Hall and the Wild Wood, a secret garden in Yorkshire, a Kensington nursery where a Newfoundland dog is the nanny . . .

What a reader hopes for when he opens a book is that he will be drawn into such a place – a place that seems real – that he will be drawn into a group with a sense of community where he can feel at home. You, as the author, have to be sure what the place is like, and to convey this to the reader you use *details* and *description*.

It is the details of life at Hogwarts in the Harry Potter books that make it a place we feel we know. It's not just the adventures and the games of quidditch, it's the details about the food they eat, the lessons they take and the whole magic ambience. We feel that if we were set down there, we could find our way to the Gryffindor common room and would recognise everyone assembled there.

Eudora Welty said, 'Time and place make the framework that any story's built on.' So, when and where you set your story is of the utmost importance and, depending on the story you have in mind, you have several choices.

HERE AND NOW

If you are writing a contemporary story about children and their family, or children and their school friends, you can either make up a place or use somewhere you know well.

◆ If you use a real place, be sure to get the details right. Don't put the town hall on the wrong side of the street, for instance, or you will get letters from readers gleefully pointing out your error.

◆ If you make up a place, you still have to be careful about the details because as you describe it, your readers will get to know it. You might find it useful to draw yourself a map of the area or a plan of the town, so your characters behave feasibly. You don't want them running from the bakery to John's house in two minutes when earlier you have established that the two places are a mile apart. Be consistent.

◆ If you know an area well but don't want to use a particular town or village, you can invent and name a village but set in that locality, placing it by naming a big town nearby or mentioning the river that runs through the neighbourhood. Thus you have the best of both worlds – a locality you know and can describe, but a village about which only you know the details and layout.

◆ You may find it helpful to draw a plan of houses and other buildings in which your story takes place, marking doorways, staircases and windows. Look for places where things could go wrong (a door that opens outward instead of inward where someone could be knocked out; a short flight of stairs someone could trip on; an old trapdoor covered by a rug which someone could fall through). Something like this could be valuable when you want an incident to ratchet up the tension.

A MAGICAL WORLD

With magic it would seem that anything goes, but be warned. You need to plan the details of the setting just as carefully as you do for a real place. You have to establish parameters of the magic and stick with them. You can create any kind of world, with any kind of rules, no matter how strange, and as long as you stick to the rules of your world, your reader will follow you.

Ask yourself:

◆ How is the magic world different from ours? Is it a fairy tale kingdom?

◆ Who rules? A king or queen? Wizards or witches? Who has most power in the kingdom?

◆ Are the people exclusively human-like, or are there goblins, dwarves, trolls, dragons and other mythical creatures? Do they work with the people or against them?

Jobs

◆ Are the people warlike or peace loving? How is the country policed?

◆ What kind of clothes do people wear? Tailor-made, home-made? Is cloth homespun, factory made or imported?

◆ What foods do they eat? Do non-human species eat different foods from the people?

◆ What are the buildings made of? Wood, stone, brick, marble, metal?

◆ What is the land like? Mountains, moorland, deserts, forests, plains, rivers, lakes? Is there a sea, a coast? Is the climate and are the seasons the same as in our world, or quite different?

◆ What do the inhabitants of the kingdom use for money? Or is the economy based on barter? Is the trading done in shops or markets?

◆ How do people travel? Horseback and coaches, camels, donkeys, magic carpets, broomsticks or by a mechanical contrivance?

◆ How do they light their homes? Candles, flaming torches, a form of glow worm specially developed?

◆ Who treats sick people? Doctors, wizards, herb-women, healers?

You may not need to use all these factors in your story, especially if it is a simple one for younger children, but knowing the details will give reality and solidity to your tale. These details are like the tip of an iceberg – only one tenth shows above the surface, the rest is hidden. Some writers do their world-building before they start the story, others make up the details as they go along. If the latter is your preferred method, make sure you are consistent and don't break the rules you have already laid down.

A FUTURE WORLD

Because of the concept of space travel, you are not restricted to one world, your characters can move from one planet to another. You can take our world and imagine amazing developments in government, buildings, travel and so on, making it a superior society, or you can postulate some calamity that caused a breakdown of the infrastructure of the world and a consequent return to more primitive times. You get to decide what survives and what has to be reinvented to create your world. Many of the questions above asked about the magical world apply to future worlds, especially those about the economy, who is in charge, the terrain and the climate.

WATCHPOINT

In both magical worlds and future worlds, don't have things so different from our world that the reader cannot relate to them. If you invent animals, mix some recognisable animals with them. Have barins and milchers, along with horses and goats. The same goes for plants and trees. By all means have hegler trees, bachon flowers and tanglethorns, but have willows, daisies and thistles growing beside them.

HISTORICAL STORIES

You need to do a lot of reading and research on the internet to get your historical background right. In a way you are lucky because the facts are all there for the finding, but unlucky too, because you need to be accurate. If you were to dress a lady in a henin with a veil, a dress with a ruff and farthingale and a pair of Doc Marten boots, you would have mixed so many periods that the reader would lose all confidence in your story however accurate the rest may be. Although, if you weigh your story down with too many of the unusual details that you discovered while researching, you will hold up the action, bore your reader to tears and he will consequently throw your book at the wall. As Kate Allan, one of the authors of *The Lady Soldier* by Jennifer Lindsay says; 'Period detail must enhance and not distract from the story. All the other bones of good fiction must be there.'

Try to get into the mindset of the period about which you are writing. Don't have an Elizabethan lady thinking about women's rights, for instance, or an 18th-century doctor talking about post-traumatic stress disorder. Remember how long communications took to get from one place to another when there was no reliable post, let alone telephones and email.

A magazine you may find useful for historical research and ideas is the *BBC History Magazine.*

DESCRIPTION

The problem with description is how much is enough? Readers, child readers in particular, are not fond of great chunks of description, but you need description to show where your characters are. Feed the details in little by little rather than in chunks. Set the scene by showing:

◆ What the point of view character can see; this tells readers about the character too. For instance, a football playing, outdoor kind of boy will not notice the colour and texture of curtains and rugs, whereas his older sister might well do so.

◆ Whenever you can, incorporate the description in dialogue. Instead of writing 'The castle was enormous, its grey walls looked forbidding,' try:

'Wow!' said Patty, looking up at the imposing castle, 'It's so big it quite takes my breath away. How on earth will we ever get into it?'
Geoffrey shuddered. 'Must we go in? Do we have to? I really don't like it. Those grey walls look as though they are frowning at us.'

◆ Include objects that are going to play a role in the scene, or that will become important later on; for example, a letter on the mantelpiece that has the tickets for the theatre next evening.

◆ Don't forget to use the point of view character's senses besides sight in your description – what can he smell? what can he hear?

Good description creates the illusion of reality. Here is Diagon Alley as Harry first sees it in *Harry Potter and the Philosopher's Stone:*

> Harry wished he had about eight more eyes. He turned his head in every direction as they walked up the street, trying to look at everything at once: the shops, the things outside them, the people doing their shopping. A plump woman outside an Apothecary was shaking her head as they passed, saying, 'Dragon liver, seventeen Sickles an ounce, they're mad . . .'

Description can be used to set up mood and subtext and to engage the readers' emotions. When Hagrid leads the First Years from the boats to the castle of Hogwarts, J.K. Rowling says:

> Slipping and stumbling they followed Hagrid down what seemed to be a steep, narrow path. It was so dark on either side of them that Harry thought there must be thick trees there. Nobody spoke much. Neville, the boy who kept losing his toad, sniffed once or twice.

There is a definite sense of eeriness created by the darkness and the guess at thick trees; the comment about the children not talking and Neville sniffing is subtext that adds to the feeling of unease.

Description can be used as a transitional device to link scenes or change time and place. If you finish a scene with your hero at the beach, sitting in the noonday sun, you might begin the next scene by mentioning the lengthening shadows, the chill of evening and have him walking back to the house while you describe the cliff path and the high tide. This has alerted the reader to a change of scene and time without your having to say, 'Later that day . . .'.

USE YOUR NOTEBOOK

Whenever you go to a new place, a different town, a different part of the country, or abroad, make notes of what the place is like, what your senses tell you about it – the sights, the sounds, the smells of the place. You can use these or adapt them when you are writing. If a place takes your fancy and you decide to use it as a backdrop to your story, take photos, buy postcards and guide books – they will all help you when you sit down to write.

CONCLUSION

It is worthwhile working hard to get your setting right. In many books the setting is equally as important as the characters and the plot.

6

Starting the Story

HOOKING THE READER

Mark Haddon, author of *The Curious Incident of the Dog in the Night-time* said in an interview, 'Bore children and they stop reading. There's no room for self-indulgence or showing off or setting the scene over the first thirty pages.'

In Chapter 2 I mentioned that it is important to start your story with a hook that will keep the reader reading. Donald Maass, a celebrated agent and author of *The Break-out Novel* says:

> Over and over authors bog down their beginnings with set-up and backstory. Why is that? Perhaps it is because while writing the opening chapters the novelist is getting to know his characters. Who are they? How did they get to be that way? The fact is, the author needs to know these things, of course, but the reader does not. The reader needs a story to begin.

This is what I call putting Chapter 2 before Chapter 1. As Maass says, the author sometimes needs to describe the characters and setting so he can see them clearly, so write that first chapter by all means, but put it aside and start with something riveting. You can feed the details from your discarded first chapter into the story in little snippets as you go along.

A CAUTIONARY TALE

Rosemary Laurey, an author friend of mine, recounts this story:

> At a conference attended by an agent and an editor, the agent when asked how she picked manuscripts said she read the FIRST SENTENCE. If that caught her interest, she read the next – if it didn't she put it aside. If the second sentence was interesting, she'd read the first paragraph; if not – out it went. If the first paragraph held her, she'd read the first page, if not – back to sender, and so on. The minute the story flagged or lost her interest, the submission was put aside. As she said this, the editor nodded in agreement.
>
> There was uproar from some of the audience. How could she throw submissions aside so arbitrarily? Her reply was that she'd read so many, she COULD tell in the first line or so if it was worth reading on. The editor concurred. Then someone asked, "But what if the story really gets going on the fifth or sixth page – you've passed on a great book." Her reply was that it was the author's job to start the story on the first line, not halfway through the chapter. I've always remembered that.

WHERE TO BEGIN

Begin by upsetting the status quo. Your characters are leading an ordinary life then something happens that starts them off on an adventure or a quest, or makes them realise there is something they want badly and that NOW is the moment to get it; or they can't bear the way things are a moment longer and they must make a change NOW.

- ◆ Start on a day that is different.

- ◆ Start with someone arriving – as Mary Poppins does.

- ◆ Start with a quarrel or a fight.

- ◆ Start just before, or at the moment the trouble begins.

- ◆ Start with dialogue that is interesting – something that makes the reader sit up and take notice.

- ◆ Do not give lots of backstory. It's good to keep readers guessing at first; they will read on to find the answers.

- ◆ One sentence of description or a few words about the weather can be used to set the scene, but move quickly to action.

INTRODUCING THE MAIN CHARACTERS

If possible, get your main character into the first paragraph, certainly onto the first page. Just like newborn ducklings imprinting on the first thing they see (hopefully in their case it will be the mother bird), readers imprint on the first person to whom they are introduced in a story and assume this is the person for whom they are expected to cheer. If, for some good plot reason, you cannot bring the hero in right away, have two people discussing him so that we are intrigued by him and will recognise him as soon as he appears. For example, you might write:

'There's a new family at End Cottage,' said Alvin.
'Any kids?' asked Denise, his twin.
'I saw a boy about our age get out of the removal van. He looked cool.'
'Great. Let's see if we like him. If we do we can ask him to be in our gang.'

But suppose you want to start with the villain who is, in story terms, just as important as the hero and you feel he will set the scene? You can do this, but make sure the reader realises the villain is an opponent, and have him talk about the hero in a way that makes us anxious on his behalf. Perhaps the enchanter is casting a spell which will have a dire effect on the hero. We will be on his side even though we haven't met him yet.

Don't introduce too many people on the first page of a story, otherwise your reader's head will spin and he won't remember details you want him to know. Concentrate on your main character, put him into a troubling or interesting situation and your reader will be anxious to know what happens next.

Use vivid, active verbs that create a sense of movement. Don't say, 'It was a snowy day when the children set off . . .' Say, 'Peter looked up at the snowflakes that were as big as feathers falling all around them. He stamped to bring life back to his chilled feet . . .'

GIVING THE READER THE FLAVOUR

It is important that in the opening you subtly let the reader know what kind of story it is going to be. It is no good starting with a gory fight between two of the characters unless it is to be an action story, full of incident. When the reader finds subsequently that it is all about cultivating a flower garden (I'm exaggerating here, but you get the drift) they are going to be disappointed.

- If it is a story set in the past, a few mentions of costume, weapons or customs will tell readers all they need to know to place the story.

- If there is a princess in trouble and talk of a dragon, this alerts the reader to the fact that this is a fairy tale or fantasy. For a science-fiction story, show the setting. I began *A Clone of Espers* thus:

   Matt came out of the subway, took the escalator to the elevator, rode up thirteen floors and took the automated walkway to the Biotech Institute.

SOME GOOD BEGINNINGS

All the following are good openings because they take you right into the story without any preliminary set up.

'Bother,' said the princess as the book she'd been balancing on her head crashed to the floor.

Miss Stringle picked it up and sighed as she looked at the title. 'Not again, Princess Aurelia. Perhaps you would find waving lessons easier if you practised more instead of reading these silly pony stories.'

'But I like them. And I like to be called Princess Ellie.'
Princess Ellie to the Rescue by Diana Kimpton

From the dialogue, we see that Princess Ellie is rebellious, we don't have to be told, and we guess her attitude is going to cause trouble so we read on to find out about it.

Mother taught me to be polite to dragons. Particularly polite, I mean: she taught me to be ordinary polite to everyone. Well, it makes sense. With all the enchanted princesses and disguised wizards and transformed kings and so on wandering around, you never know whom you might be talking to. But dragons are a special case.
Talking to Dragons by Patricia C. Wrede

In this, we realise at once that we are in an enchanted fantasy land and, as the narrator is talking about how to address a dragon, we guess we will meet one soon and we read on to find out what happens.

Torak woke with a jolt from a sleep he'd never meant to have.

The fire had burned low. He crouched in the fragile shell of light and peered into the looming blackness of the forest. He couldn't see anything. Couldn't hear anything. Had it come back? Was it out there now with its hot, murderous eyes?

Wolf Brother by Michelle Paver

In this, it is a day that is different for Torak and horribly so. There is a strong sense of menace and danger here which draws us into the story.

The trouble started the day Howard came home from school to find the Goon sitting in the kitchen. It was Fifi who called him the Goon. Fifi was a student who lived in their house and got them tea when their parents were out. When Howard pushed Awful into the kitchen and slammed the door he saw Fifi sitting on the edge of a chair fidgeting nervously with her striped gloves and striped leg warmers.

'Thank goodness you've come at last!' Fifi said. 'We seem to have somebody's Goon. Look.'

Archer's Goon by Diana Wynne Jones

The mention of the Goon is intriguing. We don't know what it is so we read on to find out more about it. The story seems to be set in our everyday world, but we can't be sure.

POINT OF VIEW

This is the stage at which you must decide from whose point of view you are going to tell the story.

Omniscient point of view

Quite a lot of children's stories are told in this perspective. You are God in the story and see everything; you know what everyone is thinking and can say so. You are there as the storyteller and can comment to inform the reader.

Advantages

◆ You can address the reader over the heads of the characters, telling them things the characters don't know as well as filling in the background. But you have to be careful in addressing readers. Gone are days of the 19th century when you could say things like: 'And this, dear reader, was to be his downfall.' Or say in a patronising way: 'Now, *you* wouldn't do that would you, children?' If you use foreshadowing, 'Little did he know that before the day was out, he would have to eat his words,' use this device sparingly and carefully.

◆ Omniscient point of view is useful in that you can say, 'Barminster was an old-fashioned town, full of ancient buildings with upper storeys that overhung the roadways making them dark and shadowy.' If you were in third person showing only what your point of view character could see, he would know all this because it is his home town and is so familiar that he wouldn't be thinking about it. You would have to find another way of getting this information across.

◆ You can tell the reader how Lothair reacts to Princess Daisy's remark, because you as narrator can see into both their minds, whereas if you were in third limited, you could only say what Daisy *thought* Lothair's reaction was, not always the same thing.

Disadvantages

◆ You don't get as close to the characters as you do when the story is told from a single point of view. Hearing their thoughts (interior monologue) brings you so close to the character, you feel you are him. However, a skilful writer can overcome this. Read Terry Pratchett, he writes in omniscient point of view and handles it perfectly.

◆ As Roxanne Richardson, an American writer, pointed out to me, you can use omniscient point of view to give you the zoom effect of a camera lens: you start out in a distant, omniscient point of view describing a scene. Next you focus on a character, describing him and what he is doing – still omniscient but getting nearer to him. Finally you move into a close-up, the character's point of view and tell the reader what he is thinking.

First person

This is the story that is written as if the narrator were telling what happened directly to the reader, the 'I' book. The narrator can be someone who comments on all the characters, the hero in particular – for example, Dr Watson recounting Sherlock Holmes's adventures, or it can be the main character telling the story.

Advantages

◆ When the narrator is the protagonist, you can get close to him and know all his thoughts. It is a particularly good point of view for a mystery story that the protagonist is trying to unravel. You have to choose whether your narrator is reliable or unreliable. Does he tell the truth, see it like it is? Or is he telling the story as it seems to him, only to be proved wrong in the end by the facts that are revealed? This sometimes happens when the narrator is a child who doesn't understand the adult machinations of the story.

◆ You can tell instead of showing in the first person as the judgement is the opinion of the narrator. You need not be as subtle as you would be in the third person.

Disadvantages
◆ The narrator has to be on scene for every important happening or else you have to write scenes where he overhears conversations, reads diaries and letters or is told second hand of things that happened.

◆ For first person to be successful, you have to write as your character would speak, so there is no room for literary prose here. If you can carry it off, it can work well, but you have to be careful not to slip out of your adopted persona.

◆ You have to be careful not to overuse the word 'I', it can grow wearisome.

◆ It has been said that children dislike first person stories. This is a questionable theory to which I do not subscribe.

Third person, multiple points of view

In this mode, the reader is shown only what the character from whose point of view we see the scene can see, hear only what he hears. The point of view character cannot know what the other people in the scene are thinking, he can only surmise from their reactions. But you do not have to stick to one viewpoint for the whole story, you can change your point of view character, but do not do it not within a scene, it must be in a separate scene.

Suppose you have a scene from Princess Daisy's point of view where she talks to Prince Lothair: after a scene break (a double set of spacings) your next scene can be from Prince Lothair's viewpoint and he can tell us what he thought about Princess Daisy's behaviour and he can comment (in dialogue with another character, or in interior monologue) on what she said in the first scene. After another scene break, maybe you will have a scene from Fallon, the Enchanter's point of view and he will talk about, or think about how he intends to deal with Daisy and Lothair. Then after another scene break, you will go back to Daisy.

But if you want to tell the reader what Princess Daisy said and then immediately let us know what Prince Lothair thought about it, you would be better off in omniscient point of view.

WATCHPOINT

In multiple points of view stories, 70 per cent of the scenes should be from the point of view of the main character; the other scenes should be there to illuminate the behaviour or the problems of the hero.

Third person, single viewpoint

This is seeing the whole book through one character's eyes – much like first person in that the point of view character has to be everywhere and see everything. However, you do not have to write in that character's voice, but in your own which allows you to use a more literary style.

Think carefully about how you want to tell your story and choose your viewpoint accordingly. Sometimes at the beginning of a book, I try out a scene in one viewpoint, and then in another to see which suits the story better.

TENSE

What tense are you going to write in? The majority of books are written in the past tense suggesting the story has happened and is being recounted. However, present tense is a possibility, and is particularly suited to picture books. For example:

Jane wakes up. If it is fine, she jumps out of bed. If it is raining, she snuggles under the covers. Today it is raining and Jane pulls the duvet up to her ears.

'Get up, Jane,' says Mummy. 'Breakfast is ready.'

If it were written in the past tense it would say:

Jane woke up. The sun wasn't shining so she didn't jump out of bed as she usually did. She saw it was raining and snuggled under the covers, pulling the duvet up to her ears.

'Get up, Jane,' her mother said, 'Breakfast is ready.'

My feeling is that there is more flexibility and immediacy in the present tense version but it is up to you to decide which you prefer and which suits your story better. Be careful to stick to one tense only for the whole book. Be consistent.

CONCLUSION

I cannot emphasise too strongly how important the first paragraph and the first page are. People choosing a book in a bookshop or at the library, after they have decided they like the cover, that the blurb is interesting, open the book and read the beginning. If you don't hook them right away you may have lost a sale or a library borrowing that would have helped your PLR. And as you saw from Rosemary Laurey's comments, if you don't hook the editor, there will be no book in the bookshop or the library for them to read.

7

Telling the Tale

Right. So you have got a good beginning and have hooked your reader, you have introduced your main characters and someone has a problem, or someone is in trouble. How are you going to go on? Those of you who are outliners probably know what happens next, but those who fly by the seat of their pants may be wondering.

You are going to need conflict, complications and a judicious mix of several other ingredients such as emotion and dialogue.

You are going to create scenes. You build your book with a series of scenes each having a dramatic and/or emotional effect. Every scene should have at least one change in it either major or minor, internal or external. These changes are what drives your story onto the next scene and so, forward.

WHAT IS A SCENE?

A scene is a sequence of events, that flows on from what came before and leads on to another scene.

1. You set up a situation, somebody (let's call him Joe) wants something. Will he get it? This is the scene question.

2. You bring in conflict in the shape of either:
a) someone who doesn't want Joe to have it. In nearly every scene there are at least two people who want different things, which gives you your conflict.
b) a problem which prevents him having it.

3. This causes an upset which equals trouble. Reaction to the upset which may equal more trouble.

4. A decision is made as to how to resolve the upset. The rising action should be made worse or more complicated by the choices the hero makes.

5. A new situation which may start the next scene if we stay with Joe, or be the start of a scene next time we meet him. We may interpose a scene in between from another character's point of view.

If Joe were to get a 'yes' answer to the scene question, there would be deflation of tension and the readers would think, 'That's settled', and perhaps would close the book. To keep them reading, you want them to think, 'Now what will Joe do?'

You keep on writing scenes until your tale is told. Not every scene will follow this exact pattern. Sometimes Joe will get what he wants but in getting it, a further complication will arise or a new situation will lead to a different development.

Here, to remind you, is the list of conflicts and complications mentioned earlier:

Argument

Bad weather

Death

Deflation

Denial

Disapproval

Discovery

Disillusion

Failure

Serious injury

Illness

Mechanical device fails

Mistake

Mystery

New character arrives

Opposition

Problem

Quarrel

Resistance

Surprise

TENSION

In a scene, the character's intention + the reader's anticipation = suspense. This gives you your tension. Decide what the reader will expect to happen next and think of something different. Keep surprising the reader.

Tip

A neat way to make smooth transitions from one scene to the next is to match the last thing you mention in the scene to the opening of the next one. This is something I learnt from writing radio plays. As radio is not visual but aural, you have to give listeners clues in words. Here's how it works: If Toby and Chris finish the scene deciding that they will probably be able to find out more about the Moated Grange from a book in the library, open the next scene with Priscilla (who is suspected of being up to no good) asking the librarian if there are any books in the local history section on the Moated Grange.

TALKING THE TALK

Dialogue is an important part of any story, especially children's books. You should aim to have some dialogue on every page if you can. Have you ever noticed how easy it is to skip paragraphs of narrative or long descriptions? But as soon as you come to a passage of dialogue, you are interested again and want to know what the characters say.

◆ Dialogue makes people real, gives them personality. I only ever feel I know my characters fully when they begin talking. You must not make each character talk as you do, remember that each person has his own style. Older people are more formal, children may use a lot of slang – but be careful with this. Slang goes out of fashion quickly and may date your book. Some people talk in a staccato way as if they are using verbal shorthand, others have a leisurely way of speaking. Every one has their own unique speech pattern and favourite expressions. Give your characters speech tags (a particular thing they frequently say) so that their conversation is easily distinguished from that of the others.

◆ Dialogue is an excellent way to show conflict. If two people are arguing, it sharpens up the pace of the story and reveals character. It also shows how they feel. You must always ensure that what your characters say is in keeping with their emotions at that point in the story.

◆ Dialogue in a story is not exactly like conversation in real life. The 'ums' and 'ers' should be left out unless you use them as a characteristic of one particular person – a speech tag. Listening to the radio this morning I heard a phone-in conversation in which after every few words the speaker said, 'you know' and ended his speech, 'know what I mean?' That happens in real life but you are writing fiction and need tight dialogue. Charles Dickens once said that every line of dialogue he put in his stories had been overheard by him in real life, but I am positive he did some editing to make the speeches smooth.

◆ Do not allow one character to go on talking for too long. Use interruptions which are normal in conversation. A good rule of thumb is to have a limit of three sentences. Then let somebody else have a turn at speaking. Cut dialogue to the bone – less is usually more effective – unless you are portraying a boring, wordy character such as Miss Bates in Jane Austen's *Emma.*

◆ Read your dialogue out loud to make sure it sounds natural. Check that the speech is right for that particular character. Something that looks right on the page can be incredibly difficult to say. Pay attention to that. Don't forget that many children's books are read aloud.

◆ Do without attributions ('said Harry' or 'she said') whenever it is clear who is speaking. They are seldom needed in a two-handed conversation, but in a long exchange, to avoid a list of remarks with the reader needing to count backwards to see who is speaking, occasionally put in an attribution, or better still, an action phrase that shows what the character is doing while she is talking.

◆ For attributions always use 'said'. You can never go wrong with 'said' – it is almost invisible. As Elmore Leonard wrote: 'The line of dialogue belongs to the character; the verb is the writer sticking his nose in. But "said" is far less intrusive than grumbled, gasped, cautioned, lied.' Remember you cannot 'smile/grin/laugh' a sentence. Instead you should write, 'she said with a smile/grin/laugh'.

◆ Don't qualify 'said' with an adverb to show how the speaker feels. 'He said crossly,' will not do unless the speech itself shows crossness. If it does, you don't need the adverb. An exception to this rule is when the way a thing is said is not implied by the content. ' "I am dying," she said,' is fine if it is true, but in ' "I am dying," she said jokingly', the adverb is needed.

◆ Another way to move the plot forward using speech is to have a character who talks to himself, speaking his thoughts aloud. This can be a way of conveying information to the reader and perhaps to your character who overhears the mutterer. You can convey information in dialogue as long as you do not have one character telling another something he already knows. Any piece of dialogue that starts, 'As you know, Mildred . . .' should be struck out. Do not let a character say to her brother, 'Mum says Auntie Flo, who is married to Dad's brother, Uncle Albert and lives in Brighton, is coming to stay.'

◆ What a character does *not* say can be revealing. He might ignore a question by not answering; by pretending not to have heard, or he might change the subject quickly. The reader will notice this and you will have made your point. You must decide if it suits your story purpose better for the other character to notice or not.

◆ The gestures and expressions that accompany a speech are important. If they do not match the words said it may indicate an untrustworthy speaker or merely someone who is shy. Someone who agrees with another but has his fingers curled into tight fists and his teeth gritted is obviously agreeing against his will. Use this trick to your advantage in conveying the character's thoughts as opposed to what he says. You can also have the contrary thoughts side by side with the dialogue (see page 51).

◆ As was suggested in Chapter 3, use gossipy conversation to show aspects of an absent character. Let the gossips remember times when the protagonist made mistakes or was successful. Let the reader know whether the general opinion about your main character is good or bad.

◆ Internal thoughts should be written as if the character were speaking and this counts as dialogue. Don't put internal thoughts in quotes. Another device if your main character doesn't have a friend in whom he confides is to have him talk to his dog or his horse.

◆ Beware of writing dialect phonetically. It is hard to read, and particularly difficult for children who may have only just learned the way a word is really spelled. For dialect and for foreign accents, use different speech patterns, with a few dialect or foreign words and expressions thrown in. Watch how this is handled on television and in films.

STYLE AND VOICE

You already have your own style – it is your natural way of writing – and you will find the right voice for the story as soon as you begin. For instance, if you are writing an historical novel, you may use slightly more formal language, hinting at an earlier time, than you would if you were writing a tale of contemporary schoolboys, and you might use a different voice again if you were writing a fairy tale.

WATCHPOINT

Never write in a patronising style for young children. Never talk down to them.

Your object should be to write as clearly and plainly as you can.

◆ Make 'write to express, not to impress' your watchword. When I went to college to study journalism, this was the first thing we were told to write in our notebooks.

◆ Don't use a long word if a short one will do just as well. When I was young I loved long words. I once wrote, 'After his pernoctation . . .' 'What the heck is that?' asked my editor. 'A night spent in prayer,' I said. 'Don't try to be clever, Pamela. Readers will either skip it and miss the point, or go to a dictionary and break the flow of the narrative.'

◆ Don't repeat the same word too often on a page unless you are deliberately using repetition in a book for young children. A thesaurus will offer you an alternative.

◆ Check your spelling. 'Spelling,' said Dr. Temple, a former Archbishop of York, 'is one of the decencies of life, like the proper use of knives and forks. It looks slovenly and nasty if you spell wrongly, like trying to eat your soup with a fork.' Spellcheckers are a great help but beware of using the wrong one of a pair of homonyms like *hoard* and *horde*, *troop* and *troupe*, or *staunch* and *stanch*, for instance. If you know there are two ways of spelling your word, look it up in the dictionary.

I have *The Little Oxford Dictionary* on my desk for quick reference, but I also have *The Compact Edition of the Oxford English Dictionary* (microfilmed in two volumes) for more detailed reference. You can buy *The Oxford English Dictionary* on compact disc for PCs but not, alas, for Macs.

If there are certain words that always give you trouble, it is worthwhile making a list of them in the back of your dictionary for quick reference. In mine I have words like *embarrass, parallel* and *manoeuvre*.

◆ Use punctuation correctly. *Eats, Shoots and Leaves* by Lynne Truss is not only fun to read but helpful, and http://englishplus.com/grammar/contents/html is a good online guide when you are not sure whether to use *who* or *whom* for instance.

◆ Avoid long sentences with subordinate clauses. Turn the clause into a new sentence without the conjunction.

◆ Use active verbs rather than passive ones: 'John jumped over the stile', not, 'The stile was jumped over by John.'

◆ Don't use weak qualifiers like *quite*, *really*, *fairly* or *very*. Try for a more exact word, or do without them. Mark Twain said, 'Substitute "damn" every time you're inclined to write "very". Your editor will delete it and the writing will be just as it should be.'

◆ Keep descriptions short, but use vivid language.

◆ Use details. Children like details – these are often what they remember best about a story. I confess that as a child, it was the details of food eaten by characters and the clothes they wore that I found most memorable.

THE RULE OF THREE

I have mentioned before that the rule of three is important. Think of the three bears, the three little pigs, three blind mice, the three Billy Goats Gruff, and in mythology, the threefold goddess – maiden, mother and crone. There are the three tasks a contender has to achieve before he can win the prize. You can use this rule in your fiction to give it unity and resonance.

◆ Do you remember the Bellman in Lewis Carroll's *The Hunting of the Snark*? His refrain was 'What I tell you three times is true.' Flaubert said that an object in a story has to be mentioned three times for the reader to be convinced of its existence.

◆ You can let your characters visit a certain place or do a particular thing three times, but each time escalate the interest or significance. For example:

1. Anna and James visit a scary witch to ask for help. She gives them a paper with three instructions on it. On the way home, before they have absorbed the information, the third instruction fades.
2. After doing the first two things successfully, they visit the witch again to ask about the third thing. This time she demands payment and James has to sacrifice something important to him to learn the secret.
3. They visit the witch a third time for more help. They need to know where a certain key is. This time her demand is outrageous. She terrifies them but Anna stands up to her and although she is in mortal fear, challenges her. The challenge changes the witch completely and she gives them the key they need.

◆ You can let your hero try for his goal three times and fail the first two, succeeding on his third attempt.

◆ Three characters joined in an endeavour gives you more scope for conflict and friction as each will have his own ideas and agenda.

EMOTION

Writers should not be afraid of bringing emotion into their stories. Without strong feelings a story is no more than a catalogue of events. Even in books for the youngest there should be an exploration of love, fear, envy, jealousy – all the vices and virtues (see Numbers of Things on page 199) can be used. Not all, of course, in the same story. The picture book *Guess How Much I Love You?* by Sam McBratney was a runaway success because of the love that shone from every page.

Tip
Before you write a scene, ask yourself, what emotion do I want my reader to feel as he reads this?

◆ Showing how a character feels makes him or her more real. You can show this by reactions and by internal monologues which indicate the point-of-view character's thoughts.

One of the things you should know about your main character is what he or she is afraid of. You can use this to heighten tension in a story by making it necessary for the character to face that fear in order to succeed in the quest. But you must lay the groundwork for this: early on in the story let it come out, for example, that Janet is afraid of dogs, then when one appears barring the way, the reader will know how Janet is going to feel and will be apprehensive on her behalf.

SOME FEARS

Darkness

Heights

Enclosed spaces

Crowds

Tunnels and caves

Bridges

Spiders

Snakes

Dogs

Wild animals

Water

Flying things e.g. bats & birds

THE MIDDLE OF THE BOOK

Rosemary Sutcliff said, 'At the outset there is the vision. But our struggles to translate sully the brightness. In giving it flesh some of the spirit is lost.'

'When I begin writing a book,' Jane Yolen says, 'Possibilities are limitless, or at least seem that way. This may be THE book, the one book to change the world. It is only when I hit the dreaded midsection, bogging down, mired in should-haves, that I run into trouble.'

Many writers get on splendidly for the first four or five chapters, then they hit a wall. They begin to doubt that they should be writing this book because it isn't turning out the way they think it should. They can't think what they should write next and they want to give up.

Here are ten ideas to help you get past this stage.

1. Don't go back to the beginning and tinker with it. Instead write on, even if you hate every word you are writing. It may be better than you think, and you can always change it in the rewrite. Your watchword must be – 'Don't get it right – get it written!'

2. Don't stop. The longer you leave getting on with your book, the harder it will be to get into the swing of it again. Keep on writing until you get to the end. Then you will have a rough draft that you can play with and improve.

3. If in spite of your outline, you can't think what is going to happen next, make a list of at least six things, including some that are just plain silly. Look at them hard. Could you make one of them work, or adapt it? If you have a critique partner or a close friend who is interested in your writing, pitch them the story up to the place where you are stuck and say, 'What do you think will happen next?' The answer may surprise you. A fresh mind can make you look at your story differently. When my children were young, I often used to ask them what ought to happen next. 'I've got an enclosure surrounded by a force field,' I said one day, 'How is the hero going to get through?' 'Zap it with a stun gun,' said my youngest – and it worked.

4. You don't like your main character. Are you sure he or she is the most important person in the story? Has a

minor character become more interesting? Should it be his story?

5. Would your character benefit from a name change or even a change of sex? I had a story about a boy called Ronnie which wasn't working and I couldn't think why. In desperation I changed the character to a little girl called Bonnie and it went well. *Bonnie and the Chico* sold straight away and was a great success.

6. Give your hero another character trait or a hobby he didn't have when you first conceived him. This may make him more interesting and from this characteristic or hobby a plot point may grow which will help you move on.

7. What is the weather like? If it has been sunshine all the way up to now, would a good storm clear the air and change a character's mood or perspective? Are you remembering to use all your senses in your writing as we discussed earlier? Is your manuscript full of sights, sounds, scents, tastes and textures? If not, start using them now. You can go back and put them into the earlier part you hate when you have finished the first draft.

8. Bring in another character who can stir the mixture. This can enliven a dead story. Raymond Chandler said when all else failed he always brought in a man with a gun. This is probably not what you want in a children's story, but you get the idea.

9. Is there enough emotion in the story to make the reader empathise with the characters and care about them? Have you made the villain nasty enough? Is the hero exciting enough? Do you care about the characters enough? If you don't, no one will.

10. Try one of these starter phrases, substituting the name of one of your characters for the dots, and see what happens. You can edit out the starter phrase later if it works for you.
    - In the dawn . . .
    - None of us will ever forget how . . .
    - Next day the madness started when . . .
    - It was difficult to understand why . . .
    - It was possible that . . .
    - Out of nowhere . . .
    - Where oh where had . . . gone?
    - Why oh why didn't . . .
    - Whose fault was it that . . .
    - If the fates had been with . . .

THE FIRST DRAFT

I mentioned just now that there would be a rewrite. This leads me on to another point to bear in mind in telling your tale. Some writers like to do a messy first draft, not making any changes, to get the whole story on paper, then they go back and cut, add and polish. Other writers like to polish each chapter as they go, getting it just right before they go on. I think there is much to be said for each process and probably the best way is to mix the two. Read and correct what you wrote yesterday before you begin today's work, but no more. You will still need to go through it again when you have written THE END because your ideas may have altered and something that you put in Chapter 7 will need to be foreshadowed in Chapter 2. More on rewriting in Chapter 10, Research and Revision.

8

Writing For The Younger Set

PICTURE BOOKS

Stories for 0-6 year olds with few words, anything from 500–2000 words, seem deceptively simple. Deceptively is the keyword here. In using so few words, each word must do its job, so cutting and polishing of your first draft is essential. Read as many picture books as you can to get the flavour of what is required.

◆ You have fewer than 24 pages (or 12 spreads) of text to play with. You may start with a single page, then go on to double page spreads and finish with a single page. The first page and the next two spreads set the story up, six spreads develop the story, and two spreads and the final single page tie everything together.

◆ If you are not an artist, do not worry. Your job is to supply the text and the editor(s) at the publishing house will choose an illustrator whose style they think will complement your story. Don't get an artist friend to do your illustrations unless he or she is a professional. If the publisher likes the text but not the pictures, you may lose a contract.

◆ Occasionally, you may feel you must tell the artist what should be shown in the picture to go with a particular piece of text. In that case put the instruction below the text in italics and mark it 'note to illustrator'. On the whole, it is better to allow the artist to use his or her imagination: you may find they bring something to the story you hadn't thought of.

DUMMY BOOKS

When you are satisfied with your text, fold the requisite number of sheets of paper in half and write your story on the pages as if it were a book. This way you can see how the story develops as the pages are turned. If you are doing the illustrations yourself, you can do rough sketches that go with the text. Most picture book writers do this just for themselves, but others send a tidy copy of the dummy as well as the text for the publisher to look at.

For author/illustrators: never send more than two sample illustrations with your submission, and don't send original artwork but good quality photocopies.

CONTENT OF PICTURE BOOKS

◆ Keep the story simple

◆ Use repetition, rhythm and cadence

◆ Humour is a winner with little ones

◆ Put emotion into the story

◆ Be original.

Universal themes work best as publishers always try to sell picture books to other countries to defray expensive production costs. This is why rhyming text, unless it is outstanding, is not much sought after because it doesn't translate well. Festivals that are exclusive to the UK should be avoided for the same reason. For instance an essentially English Guy Fawkes night picture book might not sell as well as one centred on Father Christmas who is recognised worldwide.

Read your text out loud. This is vital. Picture books are read many times over and must be able to stand repeating without the adult reader wanting to throw the book at the wall. This is another reason why it is essential that the story is interesting.

BEGINNING READERS

These are story books for children who have just learned to read and are usually 1500–2000 words, but check with the different publishers' guidelines, (obtainable with a query letter and a stamped addressed reply envelope). These books are illustrated, often in black and white, but again it is better to leave illustrations to the publisher.

Stories should be simple, sentences short and vocabulary easy to read and understand. Stories can be about children just like the reader; they can be about animals behaving like humans or getting into difficulties in the human world; they can be fairy tales and even simple science fiction. Use humour whenever you can. Even ghosts, witches, wizards and dragons can be offered to little ones if they are presented with humour.

Tip

Children love to laugh and they find funny characters endearing and having got to know one, will want more books about him which is good news for the author.

CHAPTER BOOKS

These are for ages 7+ who have learned to read with some fluency. They love chapter books which seem to them more like grown-up books. These can run up to 10,000 words, but again, check each publisher's series. You can have more complicated plots, use longer words and put in more characters than for beginning readers.

Use lots of dialogue and keep the story moving. Even when the characters are speaking, they should be involved in some sort of activity. A story loses its momentum when things are static.

Although you are using more words for this age group, you still need to make sure every word counts and is earning its keep. Strong characterisation is essential in all books for the younger set, it is better to overwrite the story people than have wishy-washy or cardboard characters.

You can use this format to explore problems for the young. Stories about coping with a new baby in the family; stories about visiting the doctor, the dentist or the hospital; stories about the things parents and children fight over – bedtime, bathtime, table manners and so on – are suitable subjects, especially if they are treated light-heartedly with humour.

Children this age love to read about naughty children doing things they would love to do but cannot or dare not. However, don't give them bad examples that will lead them into trouble if they follow them, otherwise you will have editors down on you like the proverbial ton of bricks. Often it is better to use animal characters in tricky situations. Children can't drive cars, for instance but an animal character like Toad in *The Wind in the Willows* can. He behaves like a spoiled child which makes reader identification even easier.

WATCHPOINT

Don't preach or let your moral show. Remember, you are writing a story not a tract. As an American publisher once said, 'If you have a message to offer, use Western Union not a book.'

SOME CLASSIC FAIRY TALE INGREDIENTS

You can use some of these to build incidents in your story. Thinking about well-known fairy tales will give you other ideas to put in the mix.

1. The hero's journey takes him through a dark forest

over a turbulent sea
or across a burning desert.

2. The hero meets
   an old woman
   a wounded animal
   or a hungry child.

If he helps them, he is given a wish or a magical object. If he refuses help, the woman/animal/child lays a curse on him.

3. To make progress, the hero has to pit his wits against
   an ugly ogre
   a hideous witch
   or a wily dragon.

If he wins, the creature is transformed into a benign helper or gives him valuable information.

4. The hero finds or is given
   a crystal ball that shows what is happening far away
   six league boots that enable him to travel fast
   or a cloak of invisibility.

If he is really lucky he may get all three.

5. The hero has to solve a riddle in order to
   get into an enchanted castle
   cross a dangerous bridge
   or pass a monster.

6. He is warned not to do a certain thing, he does it and lands him in trouble

    or he does it in order to save someone which negates the trouble.

7. The villain who wants to frustrate the hero is

    a wicked enchanter

    a spiteful sibling

    or a cross-grained witch.

THE TONE OR VOICE

Writing for the younger set should be lively and vivid, light and breezy. Solemnity doesn't go down well with this age group, they want to have fun. School is serious and hard work. In their leisure time they want to enjoy themselves, be amazed at unusual happenings, laugh at ridiculous situations.

THE END OF THE STORY

Fairy tales traditionally end, 'And they all lived happily ever after'. A happy ending is essential in books for the younger set. They need to feel that whatever has happened in the story, everything is all right now. They need reassurance, comfort and security. Often the time children hear these stories or read them themselves is bedtime, just before they go to sleep. They do not need something unsettling that will keep them awake or give them nightmares. When my eldest was at primary school he always ended the stories he wrote, 'And they all went home,' that is, to the place where children can feel safe.

It is this that Maurice Sendak so perfectly conveys at the end of *Where the Wild Things Are* when Max, having discharged his anger by cavorting and rampaging with the wild things, is attracted by the smell of good food and sails home to find his supper waiting for him in his bedroom 'and it was still hot'.

9

Happy Ever After?

THE READER'S REWARD

The ending of the book is as important as the beginning. It is
the reader's reward for having read through your story.
He wants to know how the problems you have set up are
resolved. He wants answers to the questions you have asked
throughout the book. Will Geoffrey get there in time to
rescue Esmerelda? Will the Leeson boys finally discover
what their Grandfather did that made him so disliked, and
will they be able to rehabilitate him? Will Rosy and Peter
stop the developers cutting down Blenkley Woods to make
way for a new super highway? Woe betide you if you leave
these questions hanging.

THE LAST PART OF THE BOOK

As you get to the last third of the book, fine down the issues.
Create a sense of urgency. Then just before the climax have
a *black moment* when all seems lost and your reader cannot
see how the heroes can overcome it. Then comes your big
scene – the climax, when the heroes face the villain and
finally win through.

You can stop the story there, on a note of – 'Hooray – we've won!' – or you can follow it with a final scene that gives the reader time to get his breath back, and reinforces the triumph and ties up any loose ends left over. For instance in *Charlotte's Web* by E.B. White, the triumph was when Wilbur won the medal, but Charlotte, the spider who made it all possible, dies and Wilbur is distraught until he rescues her egg sac and nurtures it all through the winter so he can have new baby spiders in his barn. The valedictory ending is perfect:

> Wilbur never forgot Charlotte. Although he loved her children and grandchildren dearly, none of the new spiders ever quite took her place in his heart. She was in a class by herself. It is not often that someone comes along who is a true friend and a good writer. Charlotte was both.

SAD OR HAPPY?

How are you going to end your book? Until recently I was sure that the way to finish a children's book was with a happy ending, or at the least a hopeful one. Then along came the Lemony Snicket books, *A Series of Unfortunate Events*, with their determination that the Baudelaire children should be unhappy. The first book, *The Bad Beginning*, starts:

> If you are interested in stories with happy endings, you would be better off reading some other book. In this book, not only is there no happy ending, no happy beginning and very few happy things in the middle.

Although this works for Lemony Snicket, I don't think it is going to change the pattern of happy and hopeful endings which most readers prefer.

ENDINGS FOR OLDER CHILDREN

As was stated in the last chapter, for the younger set happy endings are essential, but when we get to slightly older children's books, we can shade the happy ending. Your hero may not have got the thing that he wanted so badly, that started him on his quest, but he may have found something equally satisfying, he may have grown and changed and is now able to accept that there are other things that are more important. For instance, in *Anne of Green Gables* by L.M. Montgomery, when Anne finds that Marilla must sell Green Gables because she won't be able to manage alone when Anne takes up her scholarship, Anne sacrifices her scholarship and applies to be the local school teacher. But the post has already been awarded to Gilbert (*black moment*). Then Gilbert gives up his appointment so that Anne can have it, and she also gains Gilbert's friendship (*triumph and compensation*):

> Anne sat long at her window that night . . . her horizons had closed in since the night she had sat there after coming home from Queen's; but if the path set before her feet was to be narrow she knew that the flowers of quiet happiness would bloom along it. The joys of sincere work and worthy aspirations and congenial friendship were to be hers; nothing could rob her of her

birthright of fancy or her ideal world of dreams. And there was always the bend in the road!

'God's in his heaven, all's right with the world,' whispered Anne softly.

SOME WAYS OF ENDING

The end that comes full circle
The final scene is an echo of the opening scene but with the participants changed by their experiences. J.K. Rowling uses this in her early Harry Potter books.

The open end
This is when the writer intends to write a sequel or another adventure in the series and hints about it. Enid Blyton often used this type of ending. In *Five Go Adventuring Again* we read:

'No more lessons these hols!' said Anne gleefully.
'No more shutting Timothy [the dog] out of the house,' said George [a tomboyish girl].
'You were right and we were wrong, George,' said Julian. 'You were fierce, weren't you – but it's a jolly good thing you were!'
'She is fierce, isn't she?' said Dick, giving the girl a sudden hug, 'But I rather like it when she's fierce, don't you, Julian? Oh George, we do have marvellous adventures with you! I wonder if we'll have any more?'

They will – there isn't any doubt of that!

L.M. Boston did the same thing, rather more subtly and with fewer exclamation marks in *The Children of Green Knowe*:

> 'Must I go to school again next term?' Tolly asked.
>
> Mrs Oldknowe kissed him goodnight. 'I can't waste your singing on Miss Spudd any more,' she said. 'You are going to the choir school at Greatchurch. I think they may let you sing in the choir. How Alexander would have envied you! And of course all your holidays will be here. And your father has written that he wants you to learn to ride.'

For young adult books, we may take a harsher view. Robert Cormier, author of *The Chocolate War,* said in an interview, 'I don't think that having a happy ending should be one of the requirements of a children's book. Kids want their books to reflect reality, and they know that the good guys don't always win.'

The ending of Philip Pullman's *The Subtle Knife* was almost unbearably sad. Will struggles all through the book, facing challenges and deprivations looking for his father. At the moment he finds him and recognises him, his father is killed by the witch Juta Kamainen. I know of children who burst into tears at this unhappy denouement.

WATCHPOINT

Some writers are so eager to get to the end of their story that they rush what should be the most important part of the book. P.G. Wodehouse said, 'The success of every novel depends on one or two high spots. Say to yourself, "which are my big scenes?" and get every ounce of juice out of them.' And this is what you must do with your climax and ending.

GET THE ENDING RIGHT

You may have to work over your ending time and again to make it fully satisfying, just as you did with the beginning. You want your readers to close your book with a sigh because their story expectations have been fulfilled and they are sorry it is over. You want them to recommend it to their friends and you want them eager to buy your next book. None of this will happen if the ending is weak or rushed. As H.E. Bates said, 'A story is like a horse race. It is the start and the finish that count most.'

THE TITLE

You may have already decided on a title. Sometimes the title comes to you with the story idea, but if you haven't decided yet, now is the time to make your mind up.

◆ Choose something intriguing that will make the editor(s) sit up and think they want a book of that name on their list.

- ◆ Choose something that will make a reader browsing in a bookshop or library take the book down from the shelf.

- ◆ Choose something that sums up the book, is easy to say and to remember.

- ◆ Don't choose the name of the main character. *Mary Jones* is not an intriguing title. You could, however, combine her name with something that tells us a bit about the story. *Mary Jones and the Flying Bicycle* is more interesting, but even then, wouldn't you prefer to pick up *The Flying Bicycle* and wait until you got into the book to find out that its owner was Mary Jones? Michelle Paver could have called her book, the first in her series *Chronicles of Ancient Darkness*, by her hero's name, *Torak*, but it wouldn't have meant much to the reader; instead she called it *Wolf Brother* which is much more satisfying. Of course, if you establish a character that everyone wants to read about, using the name as part of the title of sequels is an advantage, for example, *Harry Potter and the . . .* (J.K. Rowling) *Paddington and the . . .* (Michael Bond).

- ◆ Titles that have a good rhythm work well – try 'ti-tum-ti-ti-tum': *The Box of Delights* (John Masefield), *The Lord of the Rings* (J.R.R. Tolkien). Alliteration is good too: *The Wind in the Willows* (Kenneth Graham), *Harrow and Harvest* (Barbara Willard), *Cart and Cwidder* (Diana Wynne Jones), *Bindi Babes* (Narinder Dhami). Karen McCombie is positively addicted to alliterative titles like *Tattoos, Telltales and Terrible, Terrible Twins; Crushes, Cliques and the Cool School*

Trip; and *Parties, Predicaments and Undercover Pets.* This rhyming title from Jacqueline Wilson is catchy: *Mark Spark in the Dark.*

◆ Titles that tell you where the story takes place are appealing, especially if it is somewhere unusual: *In the Night Kitchen* (Maurice Sendak), *At the Back of the North Wind* (George MacDonald), *Treasure Island* (R.L. Stevenson), *The House on the Brink* (John Gordon).

◆ There are certain magic words that attract children to books. I am sure you can think of dozens of titles containing the following words: *secret, hidden, magic, enchanted, dinosaur, dragon, witch, wizard, haunted, ghost.*

◆ There is no copyright in titles but if possible make sure your title hasn't been used before – or at least not lately. Go to www.amazon.co.uk and put your chosen title in the search box and see whether others come up. I recently had to change the title of a book I was working on which I had intended to call *The Frog Princess* when I found there were at least a dozen other books with that name.

◆ If you can, do away with 'A' or 'The' as the first word of your title. It will then not get lost among other A . . . or The . . . books when someone is looking at an alphabetical list of reading matter.

◆ If you simply cannot think of a title, you may have to go back to Mary Jones. On the title page of your manuscript put '*Working title – Mary Jones's Story*' and hope that you or your editor will think of something better before it goes to print.

10

Research and Revision

RESEARCH

Dr Johnson said, 'Knowledge is of two kinds. We know a subject or we know where we can find information upon it.'

BE A MAGPIE

As was said in Chapter 1, Limbering Up, reading of all kinds is essential for writers. They need to read the types of books they write, but also a variety of other books to spark their imagination. Alfred Bester said:

> The professional writer is a magpie. Ideas don't come out of nowhere, you need a compost heap for germination. I read anything and everything with magpie attention for possible story ideas: art frauds, police methods, smuggling, psychiatry, scientific research and so on. All that goes into my notebook for future use.

Articles in magazines can give you story ideas as can items in newspapers. These should be cut out and filed for reference. Story ideas can be written down on index cards and arranged in their box under headings of your choice. Often looking through them and shuffling them round can bring about a light bulb moment that starts you off on a new story.

GOING TO SEE; BOOKS AND WEBSITES

When you need to nail down a detail for your book, there are several resources open to you. Knowing where to look is half the battle when you need to do research.

◆ Books are usually my first resort because you can take your time with them and they are portable. Often, when reading up on your subject, you come across a nugget of information you didn't otherwise know, and you realise you can use it.

◆ For a book or story set in the present, you may need to know some detail about your setting – say how the bells are hung in a church tower as I did for my ghost story *The Skulls in the Belfry*. I tried several books, but the details I wanted were elusive, so I thought I had better go and look. I got permission from my local vicar to visit the bell tower of our church, made some notes and had just what I needed.

◆ Don't forget what was said in Chapter 5, Where and When. The collection of postcards and leaflets you made on trips and vacations will be useful here, along with the photos you took and the notes you made on your trips and visits.

◆ Nowadays, besides libraries, we have the world wide web and can consult a search engine such as www.google.com. We have only to type in the key words for our search and in moments we will have dozens of articles to choose from.

RULES FOR RESEARCH IN BOOKS AND ON THE INTERNET

1. Copy accurately, including punctuation. Note down the book's title, author and publisher in case you are challenged by a reader or queried by your copy editor. Keep a note of the website in the case of using the internet.

2. Wherever possible, double-check facts from another source.

INTERVIEWS

Interviewing people who have expertise is another way to tackle research. Suppose you have a character who is an archaeologist. You will get a certain amount of information from books and the internet, but if you can talk to someone whose job it is, he or she will clear up misapprehensions for you, and while listening be alert to any expressions peculiar to their profession that you can use in your character's dialogue. All professions have their own jargon.

Keep a contact book. You need a notebook indexed alphabetically like an address book, but instead of putting in people's names, put in the area of expertise. So under T you might have –

Tailor. Mr Liggens – 01398 744 900 (home number) ring in the evening.

Tea taster. Mary Allen's dad is a professional tea taster: ask her if he will answer some questions for me.

Turkish. Ayesha Bigalli, contact: ayesha@fancythat.com

As above, note in your contact book people who speak foreign languages. You may need to find a Portuguese swear word, or how to say 'thank you' in Malay. Try to have the name of a doctor, a solicitor and someone in the police. Contacts who know about horses and riding, sailing, rock climbing would be useful. Most people are usually delighted to help when you tell them the information is for a book you are writing.

Rules for interviewing

1. Make an appointment and be punctual.

2. Have a list of questions ready.

3. Make notes or use a tape recorder if your expert permits it.

4. Don't take up too much of his or her time.

5. Write afterwards thanking them for their help and remember to put his or her name in the acknowledgements.

HISTORICAL RESEARCH

◆ It goes without saying that you will read several books on your period, consult books on costume, weapons, architecture and furniture of the time. Biographies of important historical figures of your period may have insights into their childhood and give details that will help you create a boy or girl of the period.

◆ To find out what happened in a certain year, from 1758 onwards, consult *The Annual Register,* founded by Edmund Burke, which describes itself as 'A view of literature and politics of the year'. The years 1758–78 can be read online, the rest up to the year 2000 will be in reference libraries. For more recent times *The Chronicle of the 20th Century* (Longmans, 1988) is compiled from newspapers of the era, week by week. For a more general overview, try www.sbrowning.com/whowhatwhen/index.php3.

◆ You may want to create a timeline for your book to keep all the events in order. www.calendarzone.com/interactive allows you to create calendars; also you can add a certain number of days to a date and it will give you the new date.

◆ Use the bibliography which you usually find in the back of history books, biographies and some novels, to find books for further reading. Don't despise novels set in your period. Read them for atmosphere, but read critically. Although someone has already done the research, it is wise to double-check details.

◆ If you want to compare the cost of something in the past with present day values, a useful site is www.eh.net/hmit/ppowerbp. If you put in 1745 and the sum £30.3.4d it will give you the modern equivalent which may astonish you.

◆ Join a re-enactment society. Historical novelist Elizabeth Chadwick says:

> One of the ways that I do my research is through re-enactment. I would recommend it to any historical novelist as a fun way of researching their period. I feel that it adds texture and depth to the writing. Once you have been thoroughly kippered cooking a cauldron of pottage over an open fire, you know exactly what it's like and you know darned well that no one with hanging sleeves ever got cooking pot duty! I have stood on a battle field and viewed it through the eye slits of a jousting helm. I have felt the weight of a mail hauberk on my shoulders and gripped a sword in my hand. None of these experiences can be gleaned from reading a reference book. There are aspects to living history that give you an edge on historical accuracy and access to details that no one but another re-enactor can know!

REVISION

Although you have written 'THE END' at the foot of your manuscript, your work is only half done. You now have to polish your story and make it as perfect as you possibly can. It is a good idea to set it on one side for a while after finishing and do something completely different. Give yourself a break from the printed word. Do something with your hands – craft work or gardening, depending on what you like – catch up on neglected friends who you haven't had time to see during writing. Even clean and tidy your house – although for most writers I know, that is a job they hate. Then come back to the manuscript with a fresh eye.

DO A COMPLETE READ THROUGH

At this stage don't nit-pick on grammatical faults or typos – that can come later. Only make notes if something in the arc of the story seems wrong, if a scene is irrelevant or if you see a place where you have *told* the reader, not *shown* (see discussion on page 49). Find any passages of flat writing that say what you had in mind, but in a lifeless way. Either put a mark in the margin and cross-reference it with chapter and page number to a note in your story notebook, or use post-it notes to mark the places you are going to have to work on.

The beginning of the book is probably the part that will need most rewriting. Remember what was said in Chapter 6, Starting the Story about the importance of the first paragraph and the first page. This will be emphasised again in Chapter 11, Getting Published.

REWRITING

Rewrite those scenes that you have noted. Perk them up and make them sing. Once again, you have a complete manuscript and you must go through it once more, this time questioning the value of every word, every scene, every chapter. Have you got hooks at each chapter's end that will make the reader unable to put your book down? You want them to say, 'Just one more chapter, Mummy, before you put the light out.'

CUTTING

As you read through this time, use a red pen and a fine-tooth comb (to mix metaphors). Look for places where you need to/can afford to cut.

◆ Get rid of scenes that aren't relevant to the story, that don't drive the plot forward.

◆ Cut unnecessary words and phrases. Look at the adverbs. Do you need them? Look at the adjectives. Have you used too many? Can you do without any of them?

◆ Look at the verbs you have used. Look out for 'There was', 'It is'. Use 'to be' words as little as possible. Replace them wherever you can with vivid, active verbs to avoid slowing down the pace.

◆ Look at pronouns – him, her, it. Have you made it clear to whom or to what these refer? Personally I have to watch out for 'it'. You know what you mean, but will your reader?

◆ Dump dead words like *quite*, *fairly*, *rather*, *very* and *so* used as a qualifier. These make your prose wishy-washy. Be bold and assertive, give your work authority.

◆ Do you have favourite words or phrases? Are these repeated throughout the book? Check for them and vary them to avoid annoying the reader.

◆ If you are describing something, a long catalogue of 'things' confuses the reader. Remember the rule of three; three telling things about a room, a person, a scene, are often enough to allow the reader to form a picture.

◆ Be specific. How often do you hear someone say, 'Everybody says so.' This is too vague. 'A man I was talking to in the pub said . . .' is better, but, 'Mr Phipps, the vet, said . . .' carries more weight and authority.

◆ Avoid tautology (saying the same thing twice). For example, *nouns*: a baby puppy, a bouquet of flowers, new innovation; *double nouns*: Sahara Desert, cash money; *adjectives*: pure unadulterated, ashen grey; *double conjunctions*: and also, but however, *pairs*: each and every, the one and only.

◆ Are your paragraphs too long with more than one idea in them? Are your sentences varied in length? Long sentences give a leisurely feel, whereas in moments of crisis and excitement, short ones convey urgency.

CHARACTERS

◆ Check your characters for consistency. Don't have someone blue-eyed in Chapter 1 and green-eyed in Chapter 9. Is their behaviour consistent?

◆ Is their motivation clear? Is it strong enough to make them do what they have to do?

◆ Do you need all the characters? A cast of thousands is all very well for a movie, but in a book, especially a children's book, it is better to concentrate on a small number of people. If you have several minor characters who throughout the story only say a few words, can you combine two? The princess's ladies in waiting, for instance, can you combine Dorabella and Athenia and make a stronger, more interesting character? If the man in the newsagents who told Toby about the secret room in the Moated Grange doesn't have any other part to play, could you combine him with the man at the riding stables who told Toby about the owl's nest? Two bits of information from one man gives him the character trait of helpfulness and makes him more lively. Also, it is one fewer character for the reader to remember.

◆ Are there any scenes where there are several people who have nothing to say? Could you take some out or, if you must have them all, could you give them something else to say or do?

DIALOGUE

◆ Is your dialogue concise? Have you made each character's way of speaking individual? Have you used speech tags? Currently there is a character in a television show who always says, 'Yeah, but . . . no, but . . .', an excellent identifying speech tag. You don't need an attribution for someone with such a distinctive tag.

◆ Check your attributions. Have you got more than you need? Have you stuck to the almost invisible 'said'?

◆ Are any speeches too long? Remember the rule of three again – three sentences maximum and it is time for someone else to chip in.

◆ Is there phoney dialogue that doesn't advance the story, or add to character? Do away with mundane openings like an exchange of 'Good morning', 'How are you today?'

◆ Speeches starting with 'Well . . .' usually benefit from having 'well' cut.

◆ Have you used dialogue to inform the reader of something by making the characters tell each other things they already know? If so, take it out and convey the information in a different form.

◆ Have you used enough conversation? Children's books should be about 50 per cent dialogue.

NIT-PICKING

There are certain faults that are frequently seen. Some may have crept into your work. Look out for them.

◆ *Alright.* This, though often seen, is incorrect. All right should always be spelled out in full.

◆ *Less* or *few.* Wrongly used, this sets my teeth on edge. Less = quality; few = quantity.

◆ *Me* or *I.* 'I' is always the subject; 'me' is always the object. 'James and I went for a walk,' not 'James and me went for a walk.' To test this, take out James and you are left with, 'me went for a walk,' which you would never say. 'The money was left to James and me,' not 'the money was left to James and I.' Again take out James and you are left with, 'the money was left to I.'

◆ *Each other* or *one another.* Each other is between two people, one another is more than two.

◆ *Clichés.* ('Avoid them like the plague,' she said, using a cliché.) Watch out for them, eliminate them or find a fresher expression.

◆ *Exclamation marks.* Known as screamers to journalists, some of whom use them a lot, especially in headlines. In books and stories, try to avoid them. 'Help!' she cried, is a legitimate usage, but they should never be used to call attention to a joke, for instance. If a joke needs a screamer, it is not funny. Elmore Leonard in his essay describing his rules for writing, 'Easy on the Hooptedoodle'*, – said you are allowed two or three in every 100,000 words of prose.

◆ *Its* or *It's*: 'Its' is a possessive pronoun – 'the dog bit its tail.' 'It's' is a contraction of 'it is' – it's going to be a fine day.' These are frequently misused and the wrong one looks ugly.

◆ *Apostrophes*: Be careful with these. Do use them to show possession. Don't ever use them to create a plural.

◆ *Using the subjunctive.* Any clause that has 'as if' in it or 'wish' or expresses a condition contrary to fact, should

---

*I would love to print this essay in its entirety because it is so full of common sense about writing but it is copyrighted. The article was published in *The New York Times*, 16 July 2001.

take the subjunctive. 'I wish I were going to Margate,' not 'I wish I was going to Margate.' 'Suppose he were here . . . ' not 'Suppose he was here . . .'.

FINALLY

Three important points:

1. Read the whole book aloud to hear infelicities, bad punctuation and any dull bits that remain after your rewrite. Jane Yolen says:

   The eye and the ear are different listeners and in any written work, the author must satisfy both. I hear different problems when I read silently on the page than when I speak it aloud.

2. Check the spelling and the punctuation. If you are not sure how to punctuate consult a grammar book or use the grammar slammer – http://englishplus.com/grammar/contents.html.

3. Prepare a fresh typescript. How to do this is in the next chapter.

SUGGESTIONS FOR FURTHER READING

Eats, Shoots and Leaves, Lynne Truss (London: Profile Books, 2003).

Research for Writers, Ann Hoffman (London: A & C Black, 2003).

The First Five Pages: A Writer's Guide to Staying Out of the Rejection Pile, Noah Lukeman (London: Robert Hale, 2002).

Troublesome Words Bill Bryson (London: Penguin Books, 2002).

Write Right: A Desktop Digest of Punctuation, Grammar and Style, 3rd edn, Jan Venolia (Berkeley, CA: Ten Speed Press/Periwinkle Press, 1995).

Write Tight: How to Keep Your Prose Sharp, Focused and Concise, William Brohaugh (Writers Digest Books, 2002).

11

Getting Published

These are the most frequently asked questions about publication.

Q: How do I prepare my manuscript for submission?

A:

◆ Start with a title page with the title in the centre, and under it, who it is by. At the top put the type of book and number of words, for example, a children's book of approximately 20,000 words, or 20,356 words (computer count); your address, email, website (if you have one) and telephone number should be in the bottom left-hand corner.

◆ Type the manuscript in double spacing on one side of the paper only. Paper should be white A4. Coloured or tinted paper is not appreciated by editors.

◆ Do not leave extra space between paragraphs unless you want to indicate a change of scene. A little star in the margin or centre is often used between scenes in case the ending comes at the bottom of a page.

◆ Indent all paragraphs using the 'tab' key to ensure consistency, except the first line in a chapter or a new scene.

◆ Use a good, clean typeface (one with serifs, preferably). The size should be at least 12 point (10 point will give an editor who has many MSS to read eye-strain). American editors prefer Courier or Times New Roman, but English editors are less fussy as long as your font is clear and readable.

◆ Have wide margins. 1.25 inches or 3 cms all round.

◆ Number pages consecutively throughout the manuscript. Do not start again at 1 for each chapter.

◆ A header that indicates the title and author on each page is a good idea, but not compulsory. For instance, for this book I used 'Ideas/Cleaver'. This can be in 10 point so that it is not intrusive and in a different font from the main body of the text.

◆ Begin each chapter on a fresh page. Start the text a third of the way down. This white space is useful to the editor for notes to the printer.

◆ Do not have the pages bound or fastened together in any way. The typescript should be secured by an elastic band and put in a cardboard wallet folder, clearly labelled with the title, author and address. Another elastic band secures the folder.

◆ For posting, use a padded envelope, preferably a new one so that it is easy to open.

Q: How do I write a book proposal?

A: A book proposal has three parts:

◆ A cover letter

◆ A synopsis

◆ The first three chapters.

Don't forget that your book proposal should go in a cardboard folder or slip case – never a transparent plastic one as these have a tendency to slither and slide – inserted into a padded envelope to a named editor (you can check this in the reference books or by telephoning the publisher's switchboard and asking to whom you should submit a manuscript). Your proposal must be accompanied by return postage in stamps or a cheque.

Q: What should I put in the cover letter?

A: Keep it short, not more than a page. Be businesslike.

◆ Say why you are approaching this particular publisher.

◆ Give your writing record, if you have one.

◆ Distil your book in a couple of sentences. This is where the blurb I urged you to write in Chapter 2 comes in handy.

◆ Say how long the finished manuscript is.

◆ Say why it will appeal to readers; mention your target age group.

◆ Emphasise that you intend to make a career of writing, this is not just a one-off.

◆ Editor Betsy Lerner in her book *The Forest for the Trees* wrote, 'Just as the reading public judges books by their covers, we judge manuscripts by the accompanying letter.'

Q: What should I put in the synopsis?

A: This is not a chapter by chapter outline, but an overview of the book. Try to keep it to a single page, never more than two. For a synopsis, you can use 1.5 line spacing instead of double spacing.

◆ Start with the title, the theme or subject of the book.

◆ Say what age group it is written for.

◆ Say who the main characters are and mention what they do in the story.

◆ Tell the story briefly, mentioning the big scenes. Something along the lines of: 'The trouble starts when . . . the trouble gets worse when . . . the characters change when . . . all is lost when . . . but . . . saves the day and they live happily ever after.'

◆ It is important to show the ending, and tell how your characters have been changed by the adventure. Never leave the editor hanging in suspense as you would in jacket copy: he or she needs to know the resolution.

Noah Lukeman, an American agent, in his book *The First Five Pages* says:

> Agents and editors often ignore synopses; instead we skip right to the actual manuscript. If the writing is good, then we'll consider the synopsis. If not the manuscript is discarded.

This is why I emphasise so often that you must make the opening of your book count, and why I suggest you put your condensed version of the story in the cover letter.

Q: Why the first three Chapters?

A: Some writers think it would help them if they cherry-picked three good chapters from different points in the story, but it would not help their cause. The editor wants to see:

◆ Whether you have a riveting beginning which will draw in the reader.

◆ How you set up the story question.

◆ If you have lively, vibrant characters who a reader will want to follow through a book.

WATCHPOINT

Remember the importance of the first page. Look again at the cautionary tale in Chapter 6, Starting the Story. Agents and publishers are reading your manuscript looking for a reason to reject it. Don't give them any reason. Your first three chapters must be utterly compelling and/or entertaining.

Q: My book is only 3,000 words long; I don't have three chapters.

A: In the case of short books and picture books, send the whole manuscript.

Q: Suppose the publishers state they don't take unagented submissions?

A: In that case, if you feel that this is the publisher for you, try a query letter. Use the same format as that suggested for the cover letter. But end up by asking for permission to submit a book proposal. If you get the go-ahead, in the letter you send with the proposal remind the editor of her agreement, and on the outer envelope write, 'Requested Submission'.

Q: Should I send my book proposal by post or by email?

A: Never send material to an editor by email unless you have been given permission or asked to do so. It is OK to send a query letter by email. At the end of it ask if she would prefer you to send the material by post or as an email attachment. You can also ask in which format they like to receive attachments.

Q: Can I send a book proposal to more than one publisher at a time?

A: This used to be frowned upon. Nowadays when publishers take three months or more to get back to authors, it is frequently done. If you get a favourable reply and a request to see the full manuscript, you should let the other publishers know that someone is interested. This may goad them into considering your book seriously and you may end up with more than one offer. If you're doing multiple submissions, mention it in the cover letter. Put in something like: 'Please note that this is a simultaneous submission. If it is not your policy to consider simultaneous submissions, please return the materials immediately.'

Q: Why do publishers take so long to reply?

A: They receive more and more manuscripts each week and staffs are frequently quite small. If they like a submission, it often has to be read by at least three people before they come to a decision. Patience is the author's watchword here. If you harass publishers, they send manuscripts back without reading them. They do not like pushy authors.

Q: Do I need an agent?

A: An agent can be very helpful, but you can get into publishing without one. If your work is not up to snuff, agent or no agent, it will not sell. But agents don't take on writers unless they are enthusiastic about their work and think they can sell it. It is this enthusiasm conveyed to the editors that get the contracts.

It is said to be harder to get an agent than to catch the eye of a publisher. 'Getting an agent is possibly as difficult as getting a plumber on Sundays,' novelist Jim Crace wrote in a recent article. Agents prefer to take on writers who have a track record – after all they are in business to make money – so they prefer to deal with someone who not only has potential but who has already shown they can be professional and successful. If you get an offer from a publisher, that is the time to take on an agent as a member of your team.

Q: What will an agent do for me?

A: An agent can help you build a career.

- He tells you which publisher will be best for your book and sends it to them.

- He will negotiate your contract and handle the rights for you.

- He will often get you better royalties than you would get negotiating on your own.

- He will check on the progress of the book through the publishing house and get an early sight of your cover and alert you if it is not right.

- He will needle the PR people at the publishing house to get you interviews.

- He will collect your reviews, cheer with you about the good ones, comfort you about the stinkers.

◆ He will be on your side against the world.

Dotti Enderlie, author of the successful *Fortune Teller* series said:

> My agent has contact with many, many editors, and knows basically what each is looking for. She proofreads my work, makes suggestions for changes, formats it, then submits it. When it's accepted, she negotiates the contract, saving me from signing away important rights, and she also manages to get bigger advances, escalating royalties, and more contributor copies than I'd think to ask for.

For all these services an agent will take 10 or 15 per cent of what you earn in the UK and 20 per cent of foreign fees.

Q: What about e-publishing?

A: Although this is becoming better recognised nowadays for adult books, it is still not often used by writers of children's books. Few families have hand-held e-readers, and reading a download on a computer is not always convenient. Probably e-publishing of children's books is better left alone for the time being.

Q: Should I use my own name or a pseudonym?

A: There are several reasons why some writers use pseudonyms.

- Their name is the same as a well-known author and they adopt a pen name to avoid confusion.

- They have a name that is awkward to pronounce, or too long to fit comfortably on a book cover.

- They write more than one kind of book. If they use their own name for their children's books, they may want a different name if they write erotica which they would not wish children to read.

- They write six or more books a year and one publisher cannot handle them all. A different publishing house may want a different name to keep readers loyal to their house.

Q: What do I do if my book is rejected?

A: Take a deep breath and start sending it out again. See Chapter 13, If Your Book is Rejected.

Q: What do I do if my book is accepted?

A: Apart from rejoice and break out the champagne, you need to get the contract you are offered checked before you agree to do business with the publisher. If you don't have an agent, join the Society of Authors (you become eligible for membership as soon as you have a contract) and they will check it for you, making suggestions about any part they feel you should query. See Chapter 12, If Your Book is Accepted.

SUGGESTIONS FOR FURTHER READING

Children's Writers' and Artists' Yearbook, (London: A & C Black).

From Pitch to Publication: Everything You Need to Know to Get Your Novel Published, Carole Blake (London: Macmillan, 1999).

The Writer's Handbook, Barry Turner (ed.) (London: Pan Macmillan).

Always use the current edition.

12

If Your Book Is Accepted

CONGRATULATIONS! YOUR BOOK HAS BEEN ACCEPTED

After the first euphoria has died down and settled to a contented glow, I have to tell you there are still hurdles for you to jump over. You want to make sure that your book makes an impact, so take these on board.

Jacqueline Wilson, in her foreword to a book on marketing, said:

> I certainly wasn't an overnight success as a writer. I had my first book published when I was 24. For the next twenty years I wrote around 40 books. They all got published – and mostly sank without a trace. How I would have benefited from this brilliant book on marketing in those days.

The book is Alison Baverstock's *Marketing Your Book* published by A & C Black.

Here are some of the things that you still have to deal with before your book is for sale in the bookshops.

EDITORIAL SUGGESTIONS

Your editor at the publishing house will have read your book carefully and made notes on places where he thinks the story could be strengthened, cut or altered. Pay close attention to these. It may upset you that your book has not been accepted just as you wrote it, but the editor knows the market and suggestions are made because he wants the book to be the best that it can be, as do you. However, if something really goes against the grain, that you feel will alter the whole tenor of the book, argue about it. It is *your* book, after all, not the editor's. Accede gracefully if the alteration doesn't make much difference, but stick to your beliefs if it is important to you.

COPY-EDITING

The copy editor will now go through your book checking spelling, grammar and punctuation and making sure that your work is written in accordance with the publisher's house style. He will also check facts and timing discrepancies, something that it is easy for the writer to get in a muddle over, especially if there has been a lot of rewriting. The corrected manuscript should then come back to the writer for a final going over to make sure that you agree with what the copy editor has done. There may be points you want to dispute, such as the use of 'that' and 'which'. You are at liberty to dispute these points, but the commissioning editor's decision is final. If you disagree with the copy editor's corrections, write STET in the margin.

This is the last point at which you can make manuscript changes. If you leave it until you get to the proof stage, changes – even the insertion of a new sentence – can be expensive as it may mean recasting a whole chapter. Check your contract; you may be liable for the cost of major changes at proof stage.

GETTING PERMISSIONS

If you quote extensively from another author, it is up to you to get permission to do so. A brief quotation of a few lines is permissible without permission if it comes under the heading of 'fair dealing'. To get permission, contact the author's publisher not the author. You may be charged. Do not quote from a popular song or poem as this is always expensive; you will have to pay an exorbitant price for as little as two lines of a song or the use of its title.

COVER

At this stage you will probably be shown the design for your book cover. Unless it is written into your contract, you will probably not be allowed to reject it. You can, of course discuss it with your editor and it may be possible for changes to be made. I know of one case where the heroine pictured on the cover had the wrong colour hair. When the author protested, she was asked to change the text to match the illustration. Another author of my acquaintance who wrote historical novels with a military background was shocked to find his cover depicted soldiers in the wrong regiment's uniforms. He was told it was too late to change the cover

Instruction	Textual mark	Marginal mark
Insert matter shown in margin	⋏	New text ⋏
Delete characters struck through	ȼ ƀȼ	ꝺ
Close up leave characters marked	a⌒b	⌒
Change letters underlined to italic	a̲ b̲c̲	ital or ‿
Change to capital letter	a̲̲	caps or ≡
Change to lower case	Ⓐ	L.C. or ≠
Change to bold type	a̰b̰c̰	bold or ∼∼
Underline word/s	a̲ b̲c̲	underline
Wrong font: change	ⓐ	w.f. ⓧ
Invert type	ⓞ	invert ↲
Damaged character	✗	✗
Insert space	⋏	#
Insert space between lines or paragraphs	abc⎤ def	#
Transpose	⌐cd⌐ab⌐	trs or ⊔
Place in centre of line	⌈abc⌉	centre [ ]
Indent one em	⌈ab	☐
Move matter to right	⌈a bc	⌐
Move matter to left	abc⌉	⌐

Marks for proof correction.

Take over characters or line to next line, column or page	abc def	take over
Begin a new paragraph	abc	n. p. or ⌐
No new paragraph - run on	abc def	run on ⊃
Spell out in full	13	spell out
Insert full stop	⅄	⊙
Insert comma	⅄	⅄
Insert semi-colon	⅄	;
Insert colon	⅄	⊙
Insert question mark	⅄	?
Insert exclamation mark	⅄	!
Insert brackets	⅄ ⅄	c/ ⊃/
Insert hyphen	⅄	⊢⊣
Insert apostrophe	⅄	⅄
Insert single quotes	⅄ ⅄	⅄ ⅄
Insert double quotes	⅄ ⅄	⅄ ⅄
Insert ellipses	⅄	... /

and was mortified to find on publication that readers and reviewers blamed him for the inaccuracy.

Bear in mind that editors do know the sort of covers that sell books, and don't forget many people choose a book by its cover and editors know what they like.

PROOFS

You will almost certainly receive page proofs to correct, not galleys (long, thin strips of printed material) which were what we were sent years ago. Go through these very carefully, marking any errors using the chart on pages 148 and 149, Marks for proof correction. Because you know your work so well, you will probably read what you expect to see, skipping over errors if you read too quickly. The best way I know to make sure you are concentrating on the text is to use a ruler to cover all but the line you are reading. You should receive two sets of proofs, one to be marked up and returned, one also marked up, to keep for yourself. Usually the publisher asks for the proofs to be returned within 14 or 21 days.

GETTING YOUR BOOK REVIEWED

Your publisher's press officer will send your book out to the magazines and newspapers they think most likely to review your book. You can help by supplying a list of possible reviewers known to you. Perhaps you know a journalist at your local newspaper or a presenter at your local radio station. You may have contacts in the children's book world who you want to receive a copy of your book. Don't forget websites that specialise in children's books may be interested. The press officer will prepare a press release to go with the books, but you may want to prepare your own for your list of reviewers:

◆ Keep it short and sharp.

◆ Head it with an interesting selling point such as:
'Grandmother of Seven Writes Fairy Tale'
'Headmaster's Homework is Writing an Adventure Story'.

◆ Go on to say what the book is called, give your two-sentence encapsulation of the plot, state the target age group, name the publisher.

◆ Tell how Grandmother or Headmaster came to write the story.

◆ Finish with a contact person and number at the publisher and say the author is available for interview.

This is a time when it might pay to use coloured paper for your press release.

PLR – PUBLIC LENDING RIGHT

As soon as you have your publication date and your ISBN number, register for Public Lending Right. This can be a useful addition to your income. The current rate is 5.26 pence per borrowing, calculated on a system that samples libraries around the country and then averages out for the total number. Visit www.plr.uk.com to register your book, or write to Public Lending Right, Richard House, Sorbonne Close, Stockton-on-Tees, TS17 6DA.

PUBLICATION DAY

This is a very important day for you, but it is just another to publishers and journalists. Don't expect a fanfare of trumpets or bunches of flowers.

PRESS CUTTINGS

Collect all your reviews and put them in your cuttings book along with any articles your press release may have engendered. These can be useful for quoting on the cover of your next book. Put your name with inverted commas round, for example, 'Monica Smith' in Google. You may find reviews you didn't even know about.

One word of advice, if you get a bad review do not be tempted to reply to the paper or to the reviewer. Just grit your teeth and concentrate on reading the good ones.

POSTCARDS AND BOOKMARKS

Many authors have a postcard made of their book cover to use for publicity purposes. Don't forget to put on the back your ISBN number and your publisher. Send them out to all on your Christmas card list, to anyone you think may be interested. It is a good idea to send one to your local librarian and the librarian at your old school. Another useful publicity tool is a bookmark illustrating your book. Your local bookshop may agree to have a pile on the counter and to tuck one inside any children's books that are sold.

BOOK LAUNCHES

If your publisher offers you one, accept gratefully, but don't be surprised if they don't for a first book. If they host it, they will invite journalists, agents and publishers which is good for networking and you may sell some books. However, if you do a book launch privately, do it for your own pleasure and kudos. People frequently come to such events without buying the book.

BOOK SIGNINGS

These are iffy unless you are already a known celebrity. I am told it can be depressing to sit in front of a pile of books in a bookshop and not have any takers. Spare yourself this possible humiliation. However, if you speak to a writers' group or a luncheon club or make a school visit, take lots of books with you. If the audience like you, they are sure to want to buy a signed copy of your book.

SUGGESTIONS FOR FURTHER READING

From Pitch to Publication: Everything You Need to Know to Get Your Novel Published, Carole Blake (London: Macmillan, 1999).

Marketing Your Book: An Author's Guide, Alison Baverstock (London: A & C Black, 2001).

13

If Your Book Is Rejected

IT'S NOT THE END OF THE WORLD

There are very few first time authors who haven't suffered rejection so don't be downhearted. Rejection is not the end of the world; you may have a perfectly good book but have not found the right place for it yet. Remember that J.K. Rowling didn't sell *Harry Potter and the Philosopher's Stone* at her first try. Beatrix Potter, Dr. Seuss and Richard Adams all suffered rejections before they found the right niche and went on to become household names. Try not to be too upset.

If you get a standard rejection letter, prepare to send your proposal or picture book script out again straight away. If you get a rejection letter that tells you why the editor rejected it, think about what he said. You probably won't agree right away, but might he be right about what is wrong with it? Can you bear to change it? Do you think if you follow the suggestions it will improve the book?

SOME REASONS FOR REJECTION

◆ You may have chosen the wrong publisher, particularly if your rejection letter contains a phrase such as 'this is not our type of book'.

- Your book is about a dragon (let us say) and the editor has just taken on two dragon books – a third would make his list top heavy.

- Your book is old-fashioned. Are you writing with a child of the 21st century in mind? Books nowadays are sharper and edgier than they were when you were young. Have you read enough recently published books to know whether your tone is right?

- Your book is unoriginal. Is it too much like a pale copy of another book? Be particularly careful with fantasy. Editors don't want Tolkien type characters or stories too similar to *The Lord of the Rings.* Is it a Harry Potter knock-off? Although there is nothing new under the sun, you need an original slant to make your story fresh and appealing. Have you considered mixing two genres?

- Your book is too preachy. Children do not like this and they can spot from a great distance when someone is trying to 'do them good'. Leave moralising to tracts. Don't bore your reader whatever you do.

- Your book is poorly constructed and badly written. I hope that having read this book this is not the reason for your rejection. But did you send your manuscript out too soon, before you had really polished it to the best of your ability? It is no good thinking, 'It's only a children's book, that will do.' Only the very best we can do is good enough for children.

THE NEXT STEP

Go over the manuscript carefully giving it another polish and send it out again to another publisher. If you sent out a book proposal, send it again to several publishers at the same time. This applies to picture book scripts too. Don't shun small publishers. They often do an excellent job and are approachable.

A CRITIQUE PARTNER

If you have a writer friend, or meet someone on a message board to do with writing with whom you are in sympathy, you may find it worthwhile to take him or her on as a critique partner. You can make an arrangement to exchange chapters of your book and give each other helpful criticism. You don't want someone who is only going to say good things about your manuscript (although a little praise does sweeten the bargain), you want them to tell you places where your story puzzled them, places where they felt you had lost the plot and places where they were jerked out of the flow by something that jarred. Did they lose interest halfway through? Did they catch you repeating a word or phrase over and over? All this can help with your revision. You, in turn will do the same for them. Nowadays with the internet this is so easy, you just send your chapter as an attachment and it comes back with your critique partner's comments.

VANITY PUBLISHERS

Whatever you do don't fall into the trap of sending it to a vanity publisher who will charge you a huge sum of money to publish your book which will never be reviewed, because reviewers recognise the imprint and don't approve of vanity publishing. Nor will it be distributed, that will be left to you. Never pay anything to a publisher; remember, publishers pay writers, not the other way round.

SELF-PUBLISHING

The jury is still out on this, although it is respectable compared to vanity publishing. It can be a money trap and make for a lot of hard work. You will have to sell and distribute your nicely printed book to booksellers and to the public. Your garage or your spare room will be full of books and selling will take up time when you should be writing your next book. Occasionally one hears of someone self-publishing their book and then being taken up by a major publisher, but this does not happen very often.

Another disadvantage is that you will not have the services of an editor to smooth your manuscript, unless you pay privately for this service. More money spent. Self-publishing is definitely worthwhile for people who write non-fiction books on very specialised subjects with a limited market appeal, or people who are writing just for their family. If yours is a children's book of the sort we have been discussing throughout this book, you will be better off with a regular publisher.

HOW MANY TIMES SHOULD I SEND OUT MY MANUSCRIPT?

How long is a piece of string? As long as you have faith in the book and feel it is worthy of publication, *perseverance* and *patience* must be your watchwords. If you feel you have exhausted every avenue, put the book on one side and send out another. You have been writing a new book all the while you were trying to place the first one, haven't you? If not, begin at once. It will stop you worrying about the first story while you wait for replies, and if you are successful this time, you will have something new to offer to the publisher for your second book.

NEVER THROW ANYTHING AWAY

If you feel that your book has been everywhere suitable and it is time to pension it off, don't throw it away or shred it – save it. When you have achieved success you will know so much more about writing that you will be able to bring it out of hiding, refresh it, rewrite it and go on to sell it. I know several writers who wrote as many as six or eight books before they were successful, and have gone on to revive their early manuscripts and sell them.

THREE FINAL WORDS

Remember the three Ps:

◆ Professionalism – be businesslike.

◆ Patience – you need it, waiting while publishers make up their minds.

◆ Perseverance – keep on sending out query letters, proposals and manuscripts.

Good luck and may the gods of publishing smile upon you.

LISTS

I have collected oddments of information and trivia that you might perhaps want to include or refer to in the writing of your children's books. All these things can be researched in books or found on the internet, but I thought it would be useful and would save you time to have them collected together.

Let's start at the library.

At The Library

Dewey Decimal System of Book Classification

000–099	General works
100–199	Philosophy
200–299	Religion
300–399	Social sciences
400–499	Language
500–599	Pure science
600–699	Technology
700–799	Arts
800–899	Literature
900–999	Geography and history

Shelf Marks For Books About Children

155.4	Child psychology
362.7	Child care
372.21	Early childhood and education

British and American Spelling

Sometimes, American editors want you to alter British spellings to the forms they use in the US. This is not an exhaustive list, but it may help you make your alterations if you follow these patterns. The British spellings are on the left.

-our vs -or
colour/color
favourite/favorite
flavour/flavor
honour/honor
neighbour/neighbor
rumour/rumor
savoury/savory

-se vs -ze
analyse/analyze
criticise/criticize
memorise/memorize

-l vs -ll
enrolment/enrollment
fulfil/fulfill
skilful/skillful

-re vs -er
centre/center
metre/meter
theatre/theater

-ogue vs -og
analogue/analog
catalogue/catalog
dialogue/dialog

'oe' & 'ae' vs 'e'
encyclopaedia/encyclopedia
archaeology/archeology
manoeuvre/maneuver
mediaeval/medieval

-que vs -ck
cheque/check
chequers/checkers

'e' or not?
ageing/aging
judgement/judgment

-ence vs -ense
defence/defense
licence/license

Others
aluminium/aluminum
axe/ax
draught/draft
furore/furor
jewellery/jewelry
past of 'to dive' = dived/dove
past of 'to fit' = fitted/fit
past of 'to knit' = knitted/knit
past of 'to wed' = wedded/wed
plough/plow

programme/program
pyjamas/pajamas
storey/story (of building)
swathe/swath
tyre/tire
vice/vise (tool)

British and American Words and Phrases

American children's editors often ask British writers to change certain words in their books to make them more easily understood by American children. Here are some of the stumbling blocks.

British – American

aubergine – egg plant
bangers and mash – sausage and mash
bap – hamburger bun
bath – tub
bedside table – night stand
beetroot – beets
blunt (not sharp) – dull
book – reserve
boxed his ears – hit him upside the head (slang)
bicycle – pushbike
bill – check
biscuits – cookies
boiled sweet – hard candy
boiler – furnace
bonnet (of car) – hood
booking office – ticket counter
boot (of car) – trunk
braces – suspenders
broad bean – lima bean
candy floss – cotton candy
car park – parking lot

caravan – trailer
carriage (of train) – passenger car
caster sugar – superfine sugar
chemist's shop – drug store
chips – French fries
cinema – movies
coriander (herb) – cilantro
courgette – zucchini
crisps – potato chips
cupboard – closet
demerara sugar – turbinado sugar
diversion (on route) – detour
drapers – fabric store
draughts – checkers
dress circle (in theatre) – balcony
dressing gown – robe
dummy – pacifier
dustbin – trash can/garbage can
face flannel – washcloth
fancy dress – costume
Father Christmas – Santa Claus
first floor – second floor
flat – apartment
football – soccer
fringe (hair) – bangs
frying pan – skillet
galoshes – overshoes
garden – yard
gear lever (in car) – shift stick
goods train – freight train
grill (verb) – broil
ground floor – first floor
guard (on train) – conductor
guard's van – caboose
hair slide – barrette
hand brake – parking brake
holiday – vacation
hundreds & thousands – sprinkles
ice lolly – popsicle
icing – frosting

icing sugar – powdered sugar
jam – jelly or preserve
jelly – Jell-O
jug – pitcher
jumper – sweater
knickers – panties
ladder (in tights) – run (in pantyhose)
lead (for dog) – leash
lift – elevator
lollypop – sucker
loo – bathroom
lorry – truck
mince – ground meat
mobile phone – cell phone
motorway – freeway
muesli – granola
nappy – diaper
number plate – license plate
pack of cards – deck of cards
pants – underwear/panties
pavement – sidewalk
petrol – gasoline
pillar box – mail box
pinafore dress – jumper
plaster – Band-aid
porridge – oatmeal
posh – fancy
post code – zip code
pram – bassinet
pub – bar
pudding – dessert
pushchair – stroller
queue – line
reverse charges call – collect call
rubber – eraser
rubbish – trash/garbage
shop – store
shopping trolley – shopping cart
skimmed milk – low fat milk
spring onions – scallions

stall (in theatre) – orchestra seat
suspenders (for socks) – garters
swede – rutabaga
sweets – candy
terrace house – row house
throwing a wobbly – having a hissy fit (slang)
tights – pantyhose
tinned – canned
torch – flashlight
trainers – sneakers
tram – streetcar
treacle – molasses
trousers – pants
turf – sod
vest – undershirt
waistcoat – vest
wash basin – sink
washing-up liquid – dish soap
windscreen – windshield

Cherry Stones and Counting Rhymes

CHOOSING SIDES

A group of children hold out their fists. One of their number goes round the circle hitting each fist in turn saying, 'One potato, two potato, three potato four, Five potato, six potato, seven potato more.' When 'more' is struck, that fist goes behind its owner's back and the counting starts again. When there is only one fist left, that person is the chosen one.

In another counting ritual, each person is tapped on the chest while the chant is, 'Ollicker, Bollicker Suzie Ollicker, Ollicker, Bollicker, Knob.' And 'knob' goes out or is chosen. Another chant is, 'O – U – T spells out, and out you shall go, Because the king and queen say so.'

CHERRY STONES

Stones of any fruit are discarded to the words of these recipes for choosing husbands, finding when the wedding will be and how the bride will be dressed and how they will travel to the church.

◆ *(Old traditional)* Tinker, Tailor, Soldier, Sailor, Rich man, Poor man, Beggarman, Thief.

◆ *(More modern)* Soldier brave, Sailor true, Dashing airman, Oxford Blue, Skilled physician, Curate pale, Wily lawyer, Take the veil.

◆ *When?* This year, Next year, Sometime, Never.

◆ *Wedding dress:* Silk, Satin, Cotton, Rags.

◆ *Travel:* Coach, Carriage, Wheelbarrow, Dustcart.

COUNTING MAGPIES

English version
One for sorrow, two for joy.
Three for a girl, four for a boy
Five for silver, six for gold.
Seven for a secret never to be told.

Scottish version
One's sorrow, two's mirth
Three's a wedding, four's a birth
Five's a christening, six a dearth.
Seven's heaven, eight's hell
And Nine is the devil his ane sel.

COUNTING SHEEP

In different parts of the country shepherds, until quite recent times, used an old method of numbering sheep as they came through a gateway. The flock was always 'so-many score', so the numbers don't go past twenty. Each area had its own language for this. To give you the flavour, here is one set of numbers.

1	Yan
2	Tan
3	Tethera
4	Peddera
5	Pimp
6	Eddera
7	Leddera
8	Overa
9	Covera
10	Dix
11	Yan a dix
12	Tan a dix
13	Tethera a dix
14	Peddera a dix
15	Bumfit
16	Yan a bumfit
17	Tan a bumfit
18	Tethera a bumfit
19	Peddera a bumfit
20	Perio or Score

COUNTING SNEEZES

Once a wish, twice a kiss
Three times a letter.
Four times silver, five times gold.
Six times, goodness! You *have* got a cold.

Cockney Rhyming Slang

This is not a complete list, just some of the ones most often used. Often only the first word of the phrase is used, which further confuses strangers – that, of course, is what it was intended to do. I have omitted the vulgar ones – but you wouldn't use them in a children's book, would you?

Adam and Eve	believe
Apples and pears	stairs
Ball of chalk	walk
Barnet Fair	hair
Boat race	face
Boracic lint	skint (no money)
Brass tacks	facts
Butcher's hook	look
Brown bread	dead
China plate	mate
Currant bun	sun
Daisy roots	boots
Dicky bird	word
Dicky dirt	shirt
Dog and bone	phone
Dustbin lid	kid
Frog and toad	road
Jam jar	car
King Billy	chilly
Lady Godiva	fiver
Loaf of bread	head
Mince pies	eyes

Mutt and Jeff	deaf
Nervous wreck	cheque
North and south	mouth
Pen and ink	stink
Plates of meat	feet
Rosie Lee	tea
Round the houses	trousers
Rub-a-dub	pub
Ruby Murray	curry
Skin and blister	sister
Sky rocket	pocket
Syrup of figs	wig
Tea leaf	thief
Todd Sloane	alone
Tom foolery	jewellery
Trouble and strife	wife
Whistle and flute	suit

Colours of The Rainbow

When you are searching for just the right word to describe the colour of something, look no further. Here are some lists to help you.

Absence of colour
ashen
bleached
colourless
faded
neutral
pale
pale as a ghost
washed out

White/Cream
alabaster
chalk
creamy
ecru
flour
frosty
ivory
lily-white
magnolia
milky
moonstone
oatmeal
off-white
oyster

parchment
pearl white
snowy
white as a sheet
white as driven snow

Black
blue-black
coal black
dark
dusky
ebony
inky
jet
lampblack
midnight
onyx
pitch
raven
sable
sooty
black as Newgate knocker
black as ink
black as sin

Grey
charcoal
dapple grey
dove coloured
gunmetal
mousy
pearl
pewter
silver
slate
smoke
steely

Brown
bay
beige
biscuit
bronze
chocolate
cinnamon
cocoa
coffee
dun
dust
earth
fawn
ginger
hazel
kelp
khaki
mahogany
mocha
mushroom
nutbrown
roan
russet
sepia
snuff coloured
sorrel
stone
tan
taupe
tawny
walnut
brown as a berry

Red and Pink
beetroot
blood red
bloody
blush
brick red

bubblegum pink
burgundy
cardinal red
carmine
carnation
cherry red
claret coloured
cochineal
coral
crimson
fiery
fire engine red
florid
fuschia
garnet
geranium
guardsman red
incarnadine
lacquer red
lobster coloured
magenta
maroon
paprika
pillar box red
pink
poppy
raspberry
rose
rubicund
ruby
salmon
scarlet
shrimp
strawberry
sugar pink
terracotta
tomato
vermillion
wine red
red as fire

Green

apple green
avocado
bottle green
British Racing green
chartreuse
emerald
forest green
grass green
jade
leaf green
mint green
moss
olive
pea green
lime
sage green
sea green
verdant
verdigris

Yellow

amber
buff
canary
citron
corn-coloured
crocus yellow
daffodil
egg-yellow
flaxen
gold
honey
jaundiced
jonquil
lemon
mimosa
mustard
saffron

sandy
straw coloured
sunflower
sunshine yellow
topaz
yellow as a guinea

Purple
aubergine
amethyst
heliotrope
iris
lavender
lilac
magenta
mauve
mulberry
pansy
plum-coloured
puce
royal purple
violet

Blue
aquamarine
azure
baby blue
cerulean
chambray
cobalt
delft
delphinium
denim
electric blue
French navy
ice-blue
indigo
kingfisher blue
lapis lazuli

Mediterranean blue
navy blue
peacock blue
periwinkle
powder blue
Prussian blue
robin's egg
royal blue
sapphire
sky blue
turquoise
Wedgewood

Orange

apricot
brass
burnt orange
carrot
copper
flame
gold
mango
marigold
marmalade
peach
satsuma
tangerine

Mixed colours

brindled
checked
dappled
dotted
harlequin
iridescent
kaleidoscopic
marbled
mottled
multi-coloured

parti-coloured
patchwork
pied
plaid
polychrome
prismatic
rainbow
shot
speckled
spotted
striped
tartan
variegated

Heraldic colours
argent – white
azure – blue
gules – red
or – yellow
purpure – purple
sable – black
sanguin – blood red
tenné – tawny
vert – green

Contagious/Infectious Illnesses

You may want to use a childhood illness in your story to create complications. Here is a list of the most common, showing when they are 'catching' and how long your characters will be quarantined.

CHICKEN POX

Symptoms start two weeks after exposure, but can be 11–21 days. Contagious 1–2 days before rash appears, through five days after first crop of blisters. Non-infectious once all blisters have dried up. Children should be excluded from school until then.

DIPHTHERIA

Symptoms appear 2–5 days after exposure. Contagious for two weeks, but less if antibiotics are administered.

GERMAN MEASLES

Symptoms start 16–18 days after exposure but onset can be 14–23 days. Contagious from seven days before to seven days after onset of rash.

MEASLES

Symptoms appear 10 days after exposure. Rash follows in 3–7 days. Contagious from just before first symptoms appear to four days after onset.

MUMPS

Symptoms appear 18 days after infection but onset can be 12–25 days. Infectious until swelling abates.

VIRAL MENINGITIS

Symptoms occur within seven days of infection. Someone with viral meningitis should be excluded from school and contact with other children until passed fit by a physician.

WHOOPING COUGH

Symptoms appear 7–10 days after exposure. Contagious from onset of symptoms to three weeks after the onset of the coughing fits.

A paediatric intern with whom I checked these details said:

We can vaccinate children against varicella (chicken pox), measles, mumps, rubella (German measles), diphtheria and pertussis (whooping cough). We almost never see children with measles, mumps*, rubella or diphtheria because of immunisation. Pertussis immunity, however, declines after 7-10 years and children can be reinfected as adults or adolescents. Whooping cough can last for six weeks of coughing. Chicken pox immunisation is still not required by schools, and the vaccine was only introduced about 10 years ago, so adolescent children still carry risk of having chicken pox if they are exposed and have not been vaccinated. However, if your story takes place 100 years ago, all bets are off.

*Note that in 2005 the incidence of mumps in the UK rose sharply because teenagers had missed out on the MMR vaccination.

Converting Imperial to Metric, Metric to Imperial

Some of these are exact, some approximate but serviceably close.

To change	into	do this
Temperature		
centigrade	fahrenheit	add 40, divide by 5, multiply by 9 and subtract 40
Linear measurement		
acres	hectares	multiply by 0.4047
acres	square miles	divide by 640
centimetres	feet	divide by 30.48
centimetres	inches	divide by 2.54
feet	centimetres	multiply by 30.48
feet	metres	multiply by 0.3048
hectares	acres	multiply by 2.471
miles	kilometres	multiply 1.609
Mass		
grams	ounces	divide by 28.35
kilograms	ounces	multiply by 35.3
kilograms	pounds	multiply by 2.2046

Liquid measures

litres	UK gallons	multiply by 0.2200
litres	US gallons	multiply by 0.2642
litres	UK pints	multiply by 1.760
litres	US pints	multiply by 2.113
UK pints	US pints	multiply by 1.201
UK fluid ounces	US fluid ounces	multiply by 0.961
UK gallons	US gallons	multiply by 1.2009

Emoticons and Acronyms

As used in emails and text messages.

EMOTICONS

:-)	Happy or hello
^_^	Smiling
:-(	Sad or frowning
;-)	Winking
:-o	Wow!
:-I	Angry
8-)	Wearing glasses

SHORT FORMS FOR EMAILS AND TEXTS

<g>	grinning
AAMOF	as a matter of fact
AFAIK	as far as I know
B4	before
BION	believe it or not
BF	boyfriend or best friend
BTW	by the way
CUL8R	see you later
D/	do
D\	don't
DEGT	don't even go there!
d-i-l	daughter-in-law
dd	dear daughter

dh	dear husband
ds	dear son
dw	dear wife
DYK	did you know
FOMCL	fell off my chair laughing
f-i-l	father-in-law
FWIW	for what it's worth
FYI	for your information
GMTA	great minds think alike
GR8	great
HTH	hope this helps
IANAD	I am not a doctor
IANAL	I am not a lawyer
IIRC	if I remember correctly
IMHO	in my humble opinion
IOW	in other words
IRL	in real life
KISS	keep it simple, stupid
LOL	laughing out loud
m-i-l	mother-in-law
msg	message
OTOH	on the other hand
PAL	parents are listening
pls	please
POV	point of view
ROFL	rolling on floor laughing
s-i-l	son-in-law: sister-in-law
SO	significant other
thx	thanks
TIA	thanks in advance
TTFN	ta-ta for now
TTYL	talk to you later
VBG	very big grin
W/	with
W\	without
WEG	wide, evil grin
WTG	way to go!
YMMV	your mileage may vary

High Days and Holidays

January 1st	New Year's Day
January 6th	Twelfth Night
February 2nd	Candlemas
February 6th	Accession of Queen Elizabeth II
February 14th	St Valentine's Day
February 29th	Leap Year Day (every 4 years)
March 1st	St David's Day (patron saint of Wales)
March 17th	St Patrick's Day (patron saint of Ireland)
March	British Summer Time Begins (last Sunday in March)
April 1st	April Fool's Day
April 21st	Queen Elizabeth II's Birthday
April 23rd	St George's Day (patron saint of England)
April	Oxford and Cambridge Boat Race (date varies)
May 29th	Oak Apple Day
1st Monday	May Bank Holiday
Last Monday	Spring Bank Holiday
June	Queen's Official Birthday (date varies)
June	Derby Day (date varies)
June 24th	Midsummer Day
July 4th	Independence Day in the United States
July 15th	St Swithin's Day

August, Last Monday	August Bank Holiday
September 29th	Michaelmas – St Michael's Day
October 12th	Columbus' Day
October 21st	Trafalgar Day
October 31st	Halloween
October	Greenwich Mean Time Restored (last Sunday in month)
November 1st	All Saints Day
November 2nd	All Souls Day
November 5th	Guy Fawkes' Day – Bonfire Night
November 11th	Armistice Day – Remembrance Day
November 30th	St Andrew's Day (patron saint of Scotland)
November	Lord Mayor's Show in London (date varies)
November	Remembrance Sunday (nearest Sunday to 11th)
November	Thanksgiving Day in the US (last Thursday in November)
December 6th	St Nicholas' Day (in some countries Santa brings presents)
December 24th	Christmas Eve
December 25th	Christmas Day
December 26th	Boxing Day
December 31st	New Year's Eve

Easter is a variable feast. Easter Day is the first Sunday after the full moon that occurs on, or next after the Vernal equinox taken as March 21st, consequently Good Friday, Ascension Day and Whit Sunday are all variable, depending on the date of Easter Sunday.

Kings and Queens
of England

Monarch, Nickname	Dates of Reign	Spouse
William I, the Conqueror	1066–1087	Matilda of Flanders
William II, Rufus	1087–1100	(unmarried)
Henry I, Beauclerk	1100–1135	Matilda of Scotland
Stephen	1135–1154	Matilda of Boulogne
Henry II, Curt-mantle	1154–1189	Eleanor of Aquitaine
Richard I, Lionheart	1189–1199	Berengaria of Navarre
John, Lackland	1199–1216	Avis of Glos. and Isabella of France
Henry III	1216–1272	Eleanor of Provence
Edward I, Longshanks	1272–1307	Eleanor of Castile
Edward II	1307–1327	Isabella of France
Edward III	1327–1377	Philippa of Hainault
Richard II	1377–1399	Ann of Bohemia and Isabella of France
Henry IV, Bolingbroke	1399–1413	Mary of Bohun
Henry V	1413–1422	Catherine of France
Henry VI, of Lancaster	1422–1461	Margaret of Anjou
Edward IV, of York	1461–1470	Elizabeth Woodville
Henry VI, of Lancaster	1470–1471	see above
Edward IV, of York	1471–1483	see above
Edward V, Prince in Tower	1483	(unmarried)
Richard III	1483–1485	Anne Neville
Henry VII, Tudor	1485–1509	Elizabeth of York
Henry VIII	1509–1547	See 'Numbers of Things' on p.201
Edward VI, Boy king	1547–1553	(unmarried)
Lady Jane Grey	1553 (9 days)	Guildford Dudley

Mary I, Bloody Mary	1553–1558	Philip of Spain
Elizabeth I, Virgin Queen	1558–1603	(unmarried)
James I (VI of Scotland)	1603–1625	Anne of Denmark
Charles I	1625–1649	Henrietta of France

Protectorate

| Oliver Cromwell (Protector) | 1649–1658 | Elizabeth Bourchier |
| Richard Cromwell | 1658–1659 | Dorothy Mayor |

Restoration

Charles II	1660–1685	Catherine of Braganza
James II	1685–1688	Anne Hyde and Mary of Modena
William III and Mary II	1689–1702	
Anne	1702–1714	George of Denmark
George I	1714–1727	Sophia of Zell
George II	1727–1760	Caroline of Anspach
George III	1760–1820	Charlotte of Mecklenburg
George IV, Prinny	1820–1830	Caroline of Brunswick
William IV	1830–1837	Adelaide of Saxe-Meiningen
Victoria	1837–1901	Albert of Saxe-Coburg
Edward VII	1901–1910	Alexandra of Denmark
George V	1910–1936	Mary of Teck
Edward VIII	1936	Wallis Warfield
George VI	1936–1952	Elizabeth Bowes-Lyon
Elizabeth II	1952–	Philip of Greece

Mnemonics

Easy ways to remember things.

COLOURS OF THE RAINBOW

Red	Orange	Yellow	Green	Blue	Indigo	Violet
Richard	Of	York	Gave	Battle	In	Vain

KINGS AND QUEENS OF ENGLAND

Willie, Willie, Harry, Ste
Harry, Dick, John, Harry three
One, two, three Neds, Richard two
Harrys four, five six – then who?
Edwards four, five, Dick the bad
Harrys twain then Ned the lad.
Mary, Bessie, James the vain
Charleys two then James again.
William and Mary, Anna Gloria,
Four Georges, William and Victoria.

DISCOVERY OF AMERICA

In fourteen hundred and ninety two
Columbus sailed the ocean blue.

LENGTH OF MONTHS

Thirty days hath September, April, June and November.
All the rest have thirty one, excepting February alone.
It has twenty eight days clear, but twenty-nine if it's leap year.

To calculate leap years, divide the number of the year by four. If it goes exactly, it is a leap year. However, if it is the start of a century (for example, 1900) it is not unless it is divisible by 400.

Nicknames of Football Teams

Boys often have favourite football teams and refer to them by their nicknames.

Arsenal	Gunners
Aston Villa	Villains
Birmingham City	Blues
Blackburn Rovers	Rovers
Blackpool	Seasiders, Tangerines
Bolton Wanderers	Trotters
Bournemouth	Cherries
Bradford City	Bantams
Brighton & Hove Albion	Seagulls
Bristol City	Robins
Bristol Rovers	Gasmen
Burnley	Clarets
Bury	Shakers
Cardiff City	Bluebirds
Charlton Athletic	Addicks
Chelsea	Blues, the Pensioners
Chester City	Blues
Coventry	Sky blues
Crystal Palace	Eagles
Derby County	Rams
Everton	Toffees
Exeter City	Grecians
Fulham	Cottagers
Grimsby Town	Mariners

Ipswich Town	Blues – the Tractor boys
Leeds United	United
Leicester City	Foxes
Lincoln City	Imps
Liverpool	Reds
Manchester United	Red Devils
Manchester City	Blues
Middlesborough	Boro
Newcastle United	Magpies
Northampton Town	Cobblers
Norwich City	Canaries
Reading	Royals
Sheffield Wednesday	Owls, Blades
Southampton	Saints
Sunderland	Black Cats
Swansea City	Swans
Tottenham Hotspur	Spurs
Watford	Hornets
West Bromwich Albion	Baggies
West Ham United	Hammers
York City	Minstermen

Numbers of Things

SEVEN WONDERS OF THE ANCIENT WORLD

The Great Pyramid of Giza
The Hanging Gardens of Babylon
The Statue of Zeus at Olympia
The Temple of Artemis at Ephesus
The Mausoleum at Halicarnasus
The Colossus of Rhodes
The Lighthouse of Alexandria

SEVEN DEADLY SINS

Pride   Greed   Lust   Envy   Gluttony   Anger   Sloth

FOUR CARDINAL VIRTUES

Prudence Justice Temperance Fortitude

TWELVE LABOURS OF HERCULES

Killing the Nemean Lion
Killing the Hydra of Lerna
Capturing the Ceryneian Hind
Capturing the Erymanthan Boar
Cleaning the Augean Stables
Killing the Symphalian Birds
Capturing the Cretan Bull
Capturing the Mares of Diomedes
Getting the Girdle of Hypolite

Getting the Golden Apples of the Hesperides
Capturing Cerberus in the Underworld

TWELVE APOSTLES OF JESUS

Andrew
Bartholemew
James
James (the brother of John)
John
Judas Iscariot
Matthew
Philip
Simon Peter
Simon the Zealot
Thaddeus
Thomas

THREE WISE MEN

Melchior who brought Gold
Caspar who brought Frankincense
Balthazar who brought Myrrh

FOUR SEASONS OF THE YEAR

Spring commences March 21st
Summer commences June 22nd
Autumn commences September 23rd
Winter commences December 22nd

Longest day is June 21st. Shortest day is December 21st.

FOUR QUARTER DAYS

Lady Day – 25th March
Midsummer – 24th June

Michaelmas – 29th September
Christmas – 25th December

NINE PLANETS OF OUR SOLAR SYSTEM (NEAREST TO FURTHEST)

Mercury
Venus
Earth
Mars
Jupiter
Saturn
Uranus
Neptune
Pluto

NINE MUSES

Clio – history
Melpomene – tragedy
Thalia – comedy
Calliope – epic poetry
Urania – astronomy
Euterpe – music
Terpsichore – dancing
Polyhymnia – sacred poetry
Erato – love poetry

SIX WIVES OF HENRY VIII

Catherine of Aragon – divorced
Anne Boleyn – beheaded
Jane Seymour – died
Anne of Cleves – divorced
Katherine Howard – beheaded
Catherine Parr – survived

ROMAN NUMERALS

I	1
II	2
III	3
IV	4
V	5
VI	6
VII	7
VIII	8
IX	9
X	10
XI	11
XII	12
XIII	13
XIV	14
XV	15
XVI	16
XVII	17
XVIII	18
XIX	19
XX	20
XXX	30
XL	40
L	50
LX	60
LXX	70
LXXX	80
XC	90
C	100
CC	200
CCC	300
CD	400
D	500
DC	600
DCC	700
DCCC	800
CM	900
M	1000

Presidents of
The United States

1789–1797	George Washington
1797–1801	John Adams
1801–1809	Thomas Jefferson
1809–1817	James Madison
1817–1825	John Q. Adams
1829–1837	Andrew Jackson
1837–1841	Martin Van Buren
1841–1841	William Harrison
1841–1845	John Tyler
1845–1849	James Polk
1849–1850	Zachary Taylor
1850–1853	Millard Fillmore
1853–1857	Franklin Pierce
1857–1861	James Buchanan
1861–1865	Abraham Lincoln*
1865–1869	Andrew Johnson
1869–1877	Ulysses S. Grant
1877–1881	Rutherford Hayes
1881–1881	James Garfield*
1881–1885	Chester Arthur
1885–1889	Grover Cleveland
1889–1893	Benjamin Harrison
1893–1897	Grover Cleveland
1897–1901	William McKinley*
1901–1909	Theodore Roosevelt
1909–1913	William Taft
1913–1921	Woodrow Wilson
1921–1923	Warren Harding

1923–1929	Calvin Coolidge
1929–1933	Herbert Hoover
1933–1945	Franklin Roosevelt
1945–1953	Harry Truman
1953–1961	Dwight Eisenhower
1961–1963	John Kennedy*
1963–1969	Lyndon Johnson
1969–1974	Richard Nixon
1974–1977	Gerald Ford
1977–1981	Jimmy Carter
1981–1989	Ronald Reagan
1989–1993	George Bush Sr
1993–2001	William Clinton
2001–	George W. Bush

* are presidents assassinated in office

Ranks in the Armed Services

It is sometimes useful to know what the equivalent ranks are in the three services.

ARMY

Field Marshal
General
Lieutenant General
Major General
Brigadier
Colonel
Lieutenant Colonel
Major
Captain
Lieutenant
Second Lieutenant
Regimental Sergeant Major
Sergeant Major
Staff Sergeant
Sergeant
Corporal
Lance Corporal
Private

NAVY

Admiral of the Fleet

Admiral
Vice Admiral
Rear Admiral
Commodore
Captain
Commander
Lieutenant Commander
Lieutenant
Sub Lieutenant
Midshipman
Warrant Officer
Chief Petty Officer
Petty Officer
Leading Seaman
Able Seaman
Ordinary Seaman

AIR FORCE

Marshal of the RAF
Air Chief Marshal
Air Marshal
Air Vice Marshal
Air Commodore
Group Captain
Wing Commander
Squadron Leader
Flight Lieutenant
Flying Officer
Pilot Officer
Warrant Officer
Flight Sergeant
Chief Technician
Sergeant
Corporal
Leading Aircraftsman
Aircraftsman

Ranks in the Police in the UK

REGIONAL POLICE

Chief Constable
Deputy Chief Constable
Assistant Chief Constable
Chief Superintendent
Superintendent
Chief Inspector
Inspector
Sergeant
Police Constable

METROPOLITAN POLICE

Commissioner
Deputy Commissioner
Assistant Commissioner
Deputy Assistant Commissioner
Commander
Chief Superintendent
Superintendent
Chief Inspector
Inspector
Sergeant
Police Constable

CITY OF LONDON POLICE

Commissioner
Assistant Commissioner
Commander
Chief Superintendent
Superintendent
Chief Inspector
Inspector
Sergeant
Police Constable

Titles and the Peerage

Should your characters move in exalted circles, you will want to get the titles right.

The nobility comprises duke, marquess (not marquis*), earl, viscount, baron. At first mention give the full title: the Duke of Snook. After that, refer to him as 'the duke'. Their wives are: duchess, marchioness, countess, viscountess; the wife of a baron is Lady Thing. Widows use their Christian name before the title, for example, Aurelia Duchess of Snook, or simply, the Dowager Duchess of Snook. A baroness in her own right is referred to as Baroness Tootle on first mention and Lady Tootle thereafter.

Baronets and knights are known by their names with Sir in front. For example, Sir Robert Uptown, referred to as Sir Robert. Wives of baronets and knights are Lady Husband's-Surname, (Lady Uptown). Dames are known as Dame Lucy Whatnot at first mention and Dame Lucy thereafter.

Eldest sons of dukes, marquesses and earls take their father's second title. For example, the Duke of Snook's eldest son may be the Marquess of Roses. Younger sons use their first name and the family name Lord Frederick Ripple (never Lord Ripple). His wife is Lady Frederick Ripple referred to as Lady Frederick. Daughters of dukes, marquesses and earls are Lady Christian-name Surname (Lady Ernestine Treadle). Whether she marries a peer or a commoner, she is always Lady Ernestine Husband's-Surname. She is referred to as Lady Ernestine.

Younger sons of earls, and all children of viscounts and barons are the Hon., although informally known as Mr, Mrs, Miss or Ms.

*A few Scottish titles are marquis rather than marquess, and some foreign dignitaries have this appellation.

When Were You Born?

WHAT DAY OF THE WEEK?

Monday's child is fair of face,
Tuesday's child is full of grace.
Wednesday's child is full of woe,
Thursday's child has far to go.
Friday's child is loving and giving,
Saturday's child works hard for his living.
But the child that's born on the Sabbath day
Is bonny, blithe, good and gay.

*It is said that a child born on the stroke of midnight will never see a ghost.

SIGNS OF THE ZODIAC

Aries	March 21st – April 20th
Taurus	April 21st – May 21st
Gemini	May 22nd – June 21st
Cancer	June 22nd – July 23rd
Leo	July 24th – August 23rd
Virgo	August 24th – September 23rd
Libra	September 24th – October 23rd
Scorpio	October 24th -November 22nd
Sagittarius	November 23rd – December 21st
Capricorn	December 22nd – January 20th
Aquarius	January 21st – February 19th
Pisces	February 20th – March 20th

BIRTHSTONES

January	Garnet
February	Amethyst
March	Bloodstone
April	Diamond
May	Emerald
June	Pearl
July	Ruby
August	Agate
September	Sapphire
October	Opal
November	Topaz
December	Turquoise

Recommended Children's Books

Those marked with a star * are recommended authors because of their popularity, the title given is just an example. + indicates it is the first of a series.

CLASSICS

Alice's Adventures in Wonderland and *Through the Looking Glass*, Lewis Carroll.

Charles Perrault's Fairy Tales.

Grimm's Fairy Tales.

Hans Christian Andersen's Fairy Tales.

The Usborne Illustrated Guide to Greek and Norse Legends, C. Evans (London: Usborne Publishing, 1992).

PERENNIALS

+ *A Wizard of Earthsea*, Ursula LeGuin (Parnassus, 1968).

Haroun and the Sea of Stories, Salman Rushdie (London: Penguin, 1993).

Mrs Frisby and the Rats of NIMH, Robert C. O'Brien (London: Puffin, 1994; first published New York: Athenaeum, 1971).

+ *Over Sea, Under Stone*, Susan Cooper (London: Bodley Head, 1984; first published 1965).
+ *Pippi Longstocking*, Astrid Lindgren (London: Puffin, 1996; first published 1954).

Stig of the Dump, Clive King (London: Puffin, 2002; first published 1963).

The Amazing Maurice and his Educated Rodents, Terry Pratchett (London: Doubleday, 2001).

+ *The Children of Green Knowe,* Lucy Boston (London: Faber & Faber, 2000; first published 1959).

+ *The Wolves of Willoughby Chase*, Joan Aiken (London: Red Fox, 2004; first published London: Jonathan Cape, 1962).

Tom's Midnight Garden, Philippa Pearce (London: Puffin, 2005).

SOME CURRENT CHILDREN'S FAVOURITES

+ *Ark Angel*, Anthony Horowitz (London: Walker Books, 2005).
+ *Artemis Fowl*, Eoin Colfer (London: Viking, 2001).
+ *Harry Potter and the Philosopher's Stone*, J.K. Rowling (London: Bloomsbury, 1997).
  + *Northern Lights*, Philip Pullman (London: Scholastic, 1999).
* *The BFG*, Roald Dahl (London: Puffin, 2001).
* *The Illustrated Mum*, Jacqueline Wilson (London: Yearling, 1999).

CHILDREN'S BOOKS MENTIONED IN THE TEXT

A Hat Full of Sky, Terry Pratchett (London: Doubleday, 2004).

Alice's Adventures in Wonderland and *Through the Looking Glass* and *What Alice Found There*, Lewis Carroll (London: Bloomsbury, 2001).

A Little Princess, Frances Hodgson Burnett (London: Penguin, 2002; first published USA: Scribner, 1905).

Anne of Green Gables, L.M. Montgomery (London: Penguin, 1996; first published UK: Peacock Books, 1964).

Archer's Goon, Diana Wynne Jones (London: Harper-Trophy, 2003; first published London: Methuen Children's Books, 1984).

Charlotte's Web, E.B. White (London: Puffin, 2002; first published London: Hamilton, 1952).

Daddy-Long-Legs, Jean Webster (London: David Campbell, 1993; first published 1912).

+ *Five Go Adventuring Again*, Enid Blyton (London: Hodder, 2001).

Guess How Much I Love You, Sam McBratney (London: Walker Books, 1994).

+ *Harry Potter and the Philosopher's Stone*, J.K. Rowling (London: Bloomsbury, 1997).

Horrible Histories Series, Terry Deary.

Horrid Henry, Francesca Simon (London: Orion Children's, 1994).

Jimmy Coates: Killer, Joseph Craig (London: HarperCollins, 2005).

Northern Lights, Philip Pullman (London: Scholastic, 1995).

+ *Princess Ellie to the Rescue,* Diana Kimpton (London: Usborne, 2004).

SilverFin, Charlie Higson (London: Puffin, 2005).

Swan Boy, Diana Hendry (London: A & C Black, 2004).

+ *Talking to Dragons*, Patricia C. Wrede (Point Fantasy, 1984).

The Adventures of Captain Underpants: An Epic Novel, Dav Pilkey (London: Scholastic, 2000).

The Amazing Maurice and his Educated Rodents, Terry Pratchett (London: Doubleday, 2001).

+ *The Bad Beginning*, Lemony Snicket (London: Egmont, 2001).

The BFG, Roald Dahl (London: Puffin, 2001).

+ *The Children of Green Knowe,* Lucy Boston (London: Faber & Faber, 2000; first published 1959).

The Chocolate War, Robert Cormier (London: Gollancz, 1985; first published New York: Pantheon, 1974).

The Curious Incident of the Dog in the Night-Time, Mark Haddon (London: Jonathan Cape, 2003).

The Final Reckoning, Robin Jarvis (London: Simon & Schuster, 1990).

The Fortune Tellers Club Series, Dotti Enderle.

+ *The Lion, the Witch and the Wardrobe*, C.S. Lewis (London: HarperCollins, 2001; first published London: Geoffrey Bles, 1950).

The Rose and the Ring, William Thackeray (New York: Harper and Brothers, 1855; several versions since then).

The Subtle Knife, Philip Pullman (London: Scholastic, 1997).

Time Stops for No Mouse, Michael Hoyeye (London: Puffin, 2002).

Where the Wild Things Are, Maurice Sendak (London: Picture Lions, 1992).

Wolf Brother, Michelle Paver (London: Orion Children's, 2004).

REFERENCE BOOKS

Best Book Guide: For Children and Young Adults (London: Book Trust, published annually).

Character and Viewpoint: Elements of Fiction Writing, Orson Scott Card (Writer's Digest Books, 1988).

Children's Literature, Peter Hunt (Oxford: Blackwell, 2001).

Children's Writers' & Artists' Yearbook (London: A & C Black, 2005).

Creating Character Emotions, Ann Hood (Story Press, 1998).

Eats, Shoots and Leaves, Lynne Truss (London: Profile Books, 2003).

From Pitch to Publication: Everything You Need to Know to Get Your Novel Published, Carole Blake (London: Macmillan, 1999).

Marketing Your Book: An Author's Guide, Alison Baverstock (London: A & C Black, 2001).

Research for Writers, Anne Hoffman (London: A & C Black, 2003).

Sticks and Stones: The Troublesome Success of Children's Literature from Slovenly Peter to Harry Potter, Jack Zipes (New York and London: Routledge, 2000).

The Annual Register of Book Values: Children's Books (York: Clique; published annually).

The Chronicle of the 20th Century (London: Longman, 1988).

The First Five Pages: A Writer's Guide to Staying Out of the Rejection Pile, Noah Lukeman (London: Robert Hale, 2002).

The Forest for the Trees, Betsy Lerner (London: Macmillan, 2002).

The Rough Guide to Children's Books: 0–5 Years, Nicholas Tucker (London: Rough Guides, 2002).

The Rough Guide to Children's Books: 5–11 Years, Nicholas Tucker (London: Rough Guides, 2002).

The Rough Guide to Books for Teenagers, Nicholas Tucker and Julia Eccleshare (London: Rough Guides, 2003).

The Seven Basic Plots: Why We Tell Stories, Christopher Booker (New York: Continuum, 2005).

The Ultimate Book Guide: Over 600 Top Books for 8–12s, Daniel Hahn, Leonie Flynn, Susan Reuben (eds), Anne Fine (Introduction) (London: A & C Black, 2004).

The Writer's Handbook, Barry Turner (ed.) (London: Pan Macmillan, published annually).

The Writer's Idea Book, Jack Heffron (Writer's Digest Books, 2000).

Troublesome Words, Bill Bryson (London: Penguin, 2002).

Twenty Master Plots and How to Build Them, Ronald B. Tobias (London: Piatkus, 1995).

Write Right: A Desktop Digest of Punctuation, Grammar and Style, 3rd edn, Jan Venolia (Berkeley, CA: Ten Speed Press/Periwinkle Press, 1995).

Write Tight: How to Keep Your Prose Sharp, Focused and Concise, William Brohaugh (Writer's Digest Books, 2002).

Useful Websites For Children's Writers

ACHUKA CHILDREN'S BOOKS UK

www.achuka.co.uk
Up to date information on children's books, interviews with authors and what's new in children's publishing.

BOOKTRUSTED

www.booktrusted.co.uk
Children's section of the Book Trust. Promotes Children's Book Week and has a comprehensive library of children's books.

COOL READS

www.cool-reads.co.uk
Reviews by children and teenagers. Find out what children really think about books!

PREDITORS AND EDITORS

www.anotherealm.com/preditors
On this invaluable site you can look up agents and publishers about whom you are not sure.

THE SOCIETY OF AUTHORS

www.societyofauthors.org
The website has details of what the society does and how to join.

WORDPOOL

www.wordpool.co.uk
Independent children's book site for parents, teachers and writers.

Index

If you want to know how . . . to exercise your ability to write creatively

'If writing is one of your favourite things and, in doing it, you wish to recapture that sense of spontaneity and fun you had in childhood – this is the book for you. Its wide variety of exercises and visualisation techniques will enable you to explore the treasures of your subconscious, revisit your childhood world of games and make-believe and bring back what you find. It also suggests ways of using time, space and equipment creatively. By combining the practical with the imaginative in this way, it will help you at every stage of the writing process. Its aim is to get you writing, keep you writing and enable you to enjoy your work to the full.'

Cathy Birch

Awaken the Writer Within
Release your creativity and find your true writer's voice
Cathy Birch

'There is a solid, practical base to this book . . . Give Cathy's methods a try, you might surprise yourself.'
– *Writers' Bulletin*

'The book exudes confidence and optimism…full of devices to make the imagination flow.' – *Alison Chisholm, BBC Radio*

'Your true writer's voice is unlikely to inhabit the realms of logic . . . this book takes you on a journey into the subconscious to help you find that voice – and use it. The results can be both amazing and satisfying.' – *Writer's Own*

ISBN 1 84528 077 6

If you want to know how . . . to be aware of copyright and law

The law is of great significance to you as a writer. It can work to your advantage or to your disadvantage. It can help you or hinder you. The best way to ensure that you get the most out of the law is to have knowledge of it. With this book you will learn what rights you have as a writer and how to enjoy them, and what obligations you have and how to comply with them. You will discover how to avoid legal pitfalls and in the event that you find yourself in a legal entanglement, how to remedy the situation.

Writers' Guide to Copyright and Law
Learn what rights you have as a writer and how to enjoy them; what obligations you have and how to comply with them
Helen Shay

'Clear, no-nonsense style . . . no jargon or waffle – just sound common sense advice.' – *Alison Chisholm, BBC Radio*

'Utterly invaluable . . . an absolute *must* for anyone putting pen to paper for publication.' – A UK reader

ISBN 1 85703 991 2

If you want to know how ... to write and sell your novel

'The old adage about writing being ninety-nine per cent perspiration and one percent inspiration is certainly true. Many a talented writer has failed to achieve full potential because of a lack of perspiration . . . or because of a lack of instruction. Writers need all the help they can get in the way of professional expertise and general advice. This book may well pinpoint just what you need to know. Read, adapt, and apply. Then try again. And don't be discouraged. If you have the one percent inspiration, it will eventually win through.'

From the Foreword by Diane Pearson; Best-selling novelist, editor at Transworld Publishers and President of the Romantic Novelists' Association

The Beginner's Guide to Writing a Novel
How to prepare your first book for publication
Marina Oliver

'. . . an excellent introduction for the new novelist.'
– *Writing Magazine*

'What I like about Marina's approach is the emphasis she places on characterisation...she shows how to make the characters compelling, how to keep the pages turning . . . The book is packed full of short and pithy tips, taking on board quotes from editors and agents. There isn't one piece of advice, one tip or suggestion for further reading that isn't full of practical common-sense.' – *Writers' Bulletin*

ISBN 1 84528 091 1

How To Books are available through all good bookshops, or you can order direct from us through Grantham Book Services.

Tel: +44 (0)1476 541080
Fax: +44 (0)1476 541061
Email: orders@gbs.tbs-ltd.co.uk

Or via our website

www.howtobooks.co.uk

To order via any of these methods please quote the title(s) of the book(s) and your credit card number together with its expiry date.

For further information about our books and catalogue, please contact:

How To Books
3 Newtec Place
Magdalen Road
Oxford OX4 1RE

Visit our web site at

www.howtobooks.co.uk

Or you can contact us by email at info@howtobooks.co.uk